Making CLASSIC TOYS that TEACH

T0265673

Step-by-Step Instructions for Building Froebel's Iconic Developmental Toys

Making CLASSIC TOYS that TEACH

Step-by-Step Instructions for Building
Froebel's Iconic Developmental Toys

Doug Stowe

BLUE
HILLS
PRESS

"For several years I sat at the little Kindergarten table-top . . . and played . . . with the cube, the sphere and the triangle—these smooth wooden maple blocks . . . All are in my fingers to this day."

   "The virtue of all this lay in the awakening of the child-mind to rhythmic structure in Nature—giving the child a sense of innate cause-and-effect otherwise far beyond child-comprehension. I soon became susceptible to constructive pattern evolving in everything I saw. I learned to 'see' this way and when I did, I did not care to draw casual incidentals to Nature. I wanted to design."

—Frank Lloyd Wright,
Frank Lloyd Wright: An Autobiography

Publisher: Matthew Teague
Editor: Kerri Grzybicki
Design: Lindsay Hess
Layout: Michael Douglas
Illustration: Carolyn Mosher, except where noted
Project and Cover Photography: Danielle Atkins
Step-by-Step and Museum Photography: Doug Stowe

Blue Hills Press
P.O. Box 239
Whites Creek, TN 37189

ISBN: 978-1-951217-08-2
Library of Congress Control Number: 2022947476

Printed in the United States of America

10 9 8 7 6 5 4 3 2 1

This book was previously published by Spring House Press. This is the first edition
by Blue Hills Press.

Note: The following list contains names used in *Making Classic Toys that Teach*
that may be registered with the United States Copyright Office:
Fallingwater; Froebel; Milton Bradley Company; TINKERTOY.

To learn more about Blue Hills Press books, or to find a retailer near you,
email info@bluehillspress.com or visit us at www.bluehillspress.com.

Contents

Classic Toys that Teach

Gifts 1 and 2 are the first gifts given to a child and are meant to begin the child's journey of development. Gifts 3, 4, 5, 5B, and 6 are the construction or building gifts, meant to increase the child's ability to construct 3D shapes. Gifts 7, 8, 9, 15, and 16 are the drawing gifts that the child can use to "draw" shapes and designs.

THINGS YOU CAN MAKE

Throughout the book, you will see sidebars showing different things you can make with each gift. Froebel developed three different ways to create arrangements with the gifts. One manner of arranging shapes is to represent objects within the child's home and family; these are called "forms of life." In this way, the gifts are used to describe and explore the child's relationships with home, community, and family. Another way to arrange the gifts is to express harmony and symmetry; these are called "forms of beauty." It was important to Froebel's idea of education that children should explore a relationship with beauty. A third way to arrange the gifts is "forms of knowledge." These forms are meant to help the child explore math and science by sorting and ordering the pieces. Between the three types of forms, children can find innumerable ways to creatively express themselves.

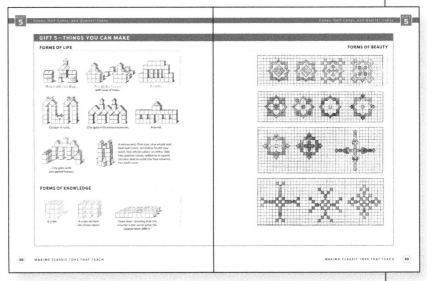

For those looking for more information about how to use the gifts, and more ideas for forms of beauty, life, and knowledge, turn to the book *Paradise of Childhood*. It is available on the Internet as a public domain PDF. The images shown in the sidebars are from this wonderful book.

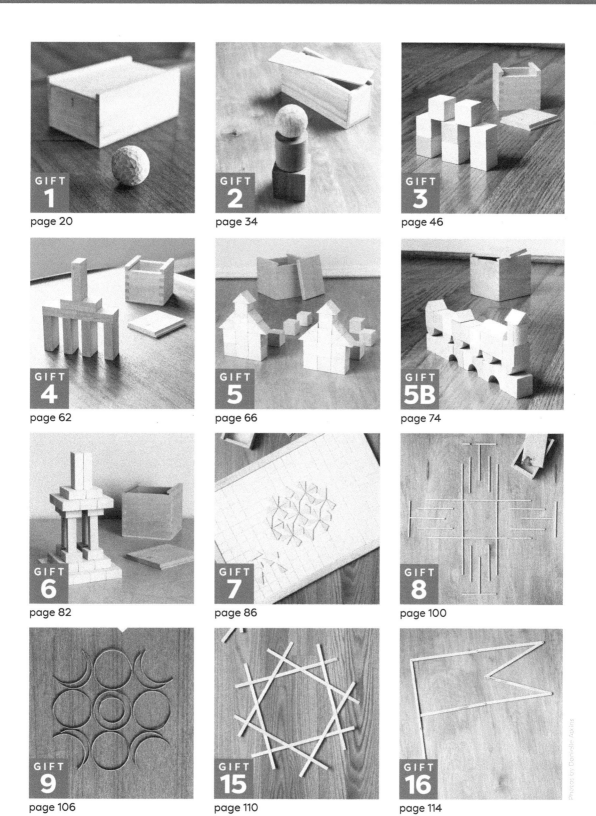

GIFT 1
page 20

GIFT 2
page 34

GIFT 3
page 46

GIFT 4
page 62

GIFT 5
page 66

GIFT 5B
page 74

GIFT 6
page 82

GIFT 7
page 86

GIFT 8
page 100

GIFT 9
page 106

GIFT 15
page 110

GIFT 16
page 114

Introduction

Nearly a century before Maria Montessori introduced her instructional objects, Froebel devised the original educational tools upon which Montessori's were based. By the time Friedrich Froebel had come up with a name for early childhood education—*kindergarten,* meaning "children's garden"—he was already an old man of 48 in a country where the average life expectancy was under 40. By the age of 48, he had started a number of relatively unsuccessful schools and had written and self-published a book with the grandiose title *The Education of Man.* The book, which Froebel only printed a few copies of in 1826, was difficult to read and understand, even in the time it was written; it received very little notice until Froebel's greater fame was made certain by his invention of kindergarten.

Froebel's contributions were a set of core principles to shepherd the development of a child's mind, accompanied by an ordered set of toys (known as gifts) to guide the child along that path—all intended to aid the child in becoming a happy, full-thinking, and productive member of his or her community. The gifts began with the simple end of the spectrum—a ball—then to a set of three blocks, and then progressed through sets that generally had an increasing number and decreasing size of pieces. As the child develops through each gift, he or she learns new ways of interacting with the world and new ways of thinking. The gifts were also designed to be used in several ways, called *forms.* There are forms of life, or arrangements of blocks that resemble items the child can see around the house or in the world at large, such as Grandpa's chair, or architectural forms; there are forms of beauty, or arrangements that are more geometrical and symmetrical, reflecting forms that might be found in nature; and there are forms of knowledge, or arrangements that guide the child through mathematical and scientific thought processes.

Before Froebel's invention of kindergarten, schools were dismal places where children learned by rote and recitation. The widespread introduction of kindergartens throughout the world showed schools and teachers a better way. Sadly, since that time, kindergarten has become too much under the influence of rigid mainstream education. Articles in educational journals have asked whether kindergarten is the new first grade; reading, writing, computer use, and standardized testing have been pushed down a grade, despite the opposition of child development specialists and knowledgeable pediatricians. This book is dedicated to showing the potential of kindergarten as originally intended by its creator.

Froebel's Main Ideas

The concepts that Froebel described in *The Education of Man* should be useful for parents and teachers hoping to make some use of this book. It laid out the basics of Froebel's theories and observations about how we learn, and how we learn best.

Historically Speaking:
The Principle of Self-Activity

Froebel likened the growth of a human being to the growth of a plant. As described by H. Courthope Bowen in his 1892 book *Froebel and Education by Self-Activity*, it was Froebel's idea that:

"To produce development most truly and effectively, the exercise must arise from and be sustained by the thing's own activity—its own natural powers, and all of them (as far as these are in *any* sense connected with the activity proposed) should be awakened and become naturally active. If, for instance, we desire to further the development of a plant, what we have to do is to induce the plant (and the whole of it) to become active in its own natural way, and to help it to sustain that activity. We may abridge the time; we may modify the result; but we must act through and by the plant's own activity. This activity of a thing's own self we call self-activity."

The First Principle: Self-Activity

Froebel believed that education should not be "one-sided": education was not only about the deliberate placing of particular knowledge in the child's consciousness, but also must be balanced by the child's outward expression of that learning. The means that the child would use to learn best and also to express learning, Froebel called *self-activity*—his first principle. Froebel viewed learning as the child's most natural and instinctive activity, not something that needed to be forced. By engaging the child's curiosity, playfulness, and natural readiness to learn, schools might become more effective than they had been up to that time. Froebel's concept of self-activity was core to building such a method of education, as were the other principles Froebel applied in his plan for schooling. By examining Froebel's gifts, an ordered set of deceptively simple playthings, these principles can be discovered.

The Second Principle: Continuity

Just as the gifts were numbered, with each leading developmentally to the next, Froebel intended that education offer a sense of continuity through all grade levels, starting with kindergarten. This second concept of *continuity* was described by H. Courthope Bowen as follows: "As that which is exercised (whether mind or muscle) grows constantly capable of higher or more varied activity, so must the exercise given grow continuously higher and more varied in character—keeping pace with the development, never outrunning it too eagerly, nor lagging lazily behind—every stage growing naturally out of that which precedes."

The Third Principle: Connectedness

Froebel's third principle was *connectedness*. While one could focus attention on facts and things in isolation, those facts and things are also deeply connected through myriad means; the child, too, should learn to see himself or herself as a part of the larger unbound world. As outlined by Froebel in *The Education of Man*, "Education should be one connected whole, and should advance with an orderly and continuous growth—as orderly, continuous and natural as the growth of a plant."

The Fourth Principle: Creativeness

Froebel called his fourth important requirement of education *creativeness*. It was not enough for a child to learn principles through self-active manipulation of various gifts. Development, from the child's point of view, involved taking in knowledge, assimilating it, and then expressing it in new forms through personal creativity. Testing a child to see if he or she could give a correct answer is not enough—to use knowledge creatively requires that the child directly test what has been learned and directly measure its effect. Creativity offers students a means to test what they have been taught, to engage in direct problem solving, and to directly observe and measure their own skill and understanding. As described by H. Courthope Bowen, "Mind-growth is aided by the mind being enabled to take in the kind of knowledge it needs, just so much of it as it needs, and just when it needs this knowledge; by its being enabled to work this knowledge up into its very self, and to use it as a means of life."

Historically Speaking:
The Principle of Connectedness

H. Courthope Bowen described the principle of connectedness this way:

"This view is considerably strengthened when we observe that, to the young child, as to primitive humanity, all knowledge does, as a matter of fact, come as one whole, and that the subdivision into subjects and departments is a very gradually evolved plan, for the most part wholly artificial, and only adopted for the sake of convenience. Moreover, the very nature of knowledge itself teaches the necessity for connectedness. Facts in isolation, and unrelated to one another, do not form knowledge. Facts have to be compared, classified, organized, connected, before they become what we call knowledge. Knowledge grows when new facts are rightly connected with facts already arranged and organized, and when the connections perceived are made clearer and clearer, and are widened and deepened and multiplied. And so, since education has largely to do with inducing the right acquirement of knowledge and the right use of knowledge, the task of the educator must largely consist in bringing out, and making clear, and maintaining the connectedness of facts and things."

Occupations

That's where Froebel's occupations came into play. The occupations were different from the gifts, in that when a gift had been played with and learned from, it was then put away in its original box, unchanged. The occupations, on the other hand, involved the child in the direct transformation of materials into new forms. Weaving, work with clay, cutting and folding paper, and work with wood involved the child in creative play. The occupations were in no way directly connected to such occupations that adults would take on in later years, but the dexterity of hand, the understanding of materials, and a grasp of the workings of the creative mind in problem solving were aspects of learning that would come into play in countless ways throughout a child's life. An important development along these lines that came after Froebel is called *educational sloyd*. *Sloyd* is a Swedish word that means "skilled or handy." This is a system of applying Froebel's principles to children older than kindergarten age by teaching them how to work with wood. For more information, see the sidebar at 19.

As magical as Froebel's gifts may have appeared when first introduced, they were only a small part of Froebel's overall scheme for learning, which maintained that children would learn best by doing things that were of value to themselves and to their families and community. So apart from the gifts and occupations as described in this book, children went on field trips through their communities and learned about the kinds of grownup occupations and their importance. Through finger play and music, children were taught to respect and celebrate the importance of diverse community members. Through walks in the woods, gardening, nature study, and the care of small animals, children were taught to have respect for all life. Froebel's book *Mother Play* included songs, finger play, and illustrations of scenes that children might witness in their own village, such as carpenters at work. Other songs celebrated the role of nature in human life. In other words, the gifts in this book offer only a glimpse into the full scope of learning presented by Froebel's kindergarten.

The page featuring the carpenter in Froebel's book *Mother Play.*

Historically Speaking:

My Interest in Froebel's Kindergarten

I became interested in Froebel's kindergarten for two distinct reasons. First, my mother was a kindergarten teacher, and even as a very young child, I noticed that made her someone special. She had been trained to offer educational experiences to her students, and to be a trained observer of their growth. My sisters and I realized that the activities provided for our growth and amusement were distinct compared to what we found in other homes. It was not in the number of toys or generosity of the parents that the difference was made clear, but the range of activities. We finger-painted, and shaped objects out of modeling clay that mother made. So while I might have been impressed by the sheer number and variety of toys my friends might have, our home was more fun.

Later, when I became a woodworking teacher, I became interested in educational sloyd, a method of woodworking education that originated in Finland and Sweden in the 19th century. I learned that the original inspiration for this special form of woodworking education was in Froebel's kindergarten. One of the original purposes for woodworking in schools, apart from the obvious need for skilled craftsmen at the time, was that the activities in the wood shop followed Froebel's prescribed "self-activity" as the means through which children would learn best. This was intended by many as the means through which the teaching methods prescribed by Froebel could be applied beyond the kindergarten years, and have a continuing impact on the whole of the child's education and life.

Photo by Danielle Atkins

A Few Words About the Projects

Froebel's gifts were intended to progress, leading the child and his or her parents and teachers on a journey of shared growth. The basic principles, associated with Froebel's friend Diesterweg and later adopted by Cygnaeus and Salomon for educational sloyd, were:

Start with the interests of the child.
Move from the known to the unknown,
From the easy to the more difficult,
From the simple to the complex,
And from the concrete to the abstract.

In the progression of Froebel's gifts, we see a steady introduction of new forms, a growing complexity, a steady increase in difficulty in the manipulation of forms, along with a movement from concrete to abstract as students use the materials to form abstract representations drawn from life or to create beauty. Also, in this progression, we can come to an understanding of "progressive education" as referring to the systematic growth of the child. The progression of gifts serves as an important illustration, with each gift providing an opportunity for more difficult construction, with greater complexity, for students already experienced in the earlier gifts. Teachers and parents were to offer the child a basic understanding of design and creativity that would lead to more abstract expression through less-structured materials as the child grew in understanding and intellect. In simpler terms: As the child grew, the proportion of engagement by the teacher would diminish. Readers will note that the first gifts are concrete expressions. The later gifts become more and more abstract, to the point that the parent and teacher needed to do nothing more than place the material in the children's hands and allow them to create and learn on their own.

I have laid out the gifts in this book in Froebel's order, but with the recognition that the gifts were altered somewhat by Froebel's followers over the years, and also that the gifts themselves were to become more abstract and less concrete as children progressed. My numbering of gifts is based on the book *Paradise of Childhood*, first published in 1869, but the numbering of gifts varied. Froebel's gifts were made (and numbered) differently in all the places and countries they were developed.

About This Book

An important point in shaping this book's content comes from one of Froebel's guiding ideas. In his presentation of gifts, Froebel was careful to keep teachers from teaching too much and robbing the child of the pleasure that comes with discovery. One example relates to gift 2—a shape that children often discover is "the doll," a human-like shape formed when the cylinder is laid first with the cube next and the sphere placed on top. Learning must never cease to amaze and surprise, and so in my own presentation of Froebel's toys that teach, I have included enough instruction, but also wanted to leave plenty for my readers to discover for themselves.

As a lifelong woodworker, I have also been primarily interested in the gifts that can be made from wood. The main focus of this book is on providing the gift of woodworking to my readers. I discovered Froebel's kindergarten through a study of educational sloyd—as previously mentioned, this is a system of teaching woodworking that was inspired by Froebel's principles (see Educational Sloyd sidebar, page 19). In 2001, I had launched a second career as a woodworking teacher in an independent school in my hometown of Eureka Springs, Arkansas. As a new teacher (but mature woodworker), I went to a conference on the East Coast where I first learned about educational sloyd. I studied it, used some of its principles in my woodworking classes in the lower grades, and presented a paper at a conference in Sweden in 2006. It was during that trip that I visited the sloyd teacher training school at Nääs. And it was there, in Otto Salomon's library, that I became aware of the very close relationship between Swedish sloyd and Froebel's kindergarten: two concepts that had taken root in the U.S. but now are either abandoned or have been so heavily modified as to be unrecognizable.

So the question arises: "If kindergarten and wood shop had meaning and value, how do we bring them back?" And the answer is not to force educational policy makers to come to their senses, but to begin to take matters and materials in our own hands. This book is intended to enable its readers to do just that. I have written much of the how-to material in this book as an exercise in sloyd.

My other goal with this book is to paint a picture of the importance of Froebel's methods and incite teachers and parents to take matters and materials in their own hands. As of this writing, my blog, Wisdom of Hands (http://wisdomofhands.blogspot.com) has had over 1 million page views and nearly one-third of its regular readers are from outside the United States. That tells me that wisdom of the hands and how we can best address learning are worldwide concerns: Still the hands, spoil the child. And what better way can there be for setting our own hands in motion than the making of gifts that launch our children toward their own creative and constructive futures?

Historically Speaking:
Educational Sloyd

DIRECTIONS FOR ELEMENTARY SLOYD

Fig. 31.

I.—PENCIL SHARPENER
Whitewood. ⅛ inch.

TOOLS
Pencil, Rule, Plane, Bench Hook.

DIRECTIONS
Wood prepared 6¼ x 1¾ inches.

1. Plane one side straight.
2. Measure width, draw line, and plane.
3. Plane one end in bench hook.
4. Measure length and plane.
5. Sandpaper with block, rounding corners.
6. Cut sandpaper, No. 1, and glue to wood.

Educational sloyd—an educational system based on tactile learning with handcrafts—was meant to fulfill children's needs for kindergarten-style learning as they passed into the upper grades. As in Froebel's kindergarten, the making of beautiful and useful things built dexterity of hand and mind, as well as character. Gustaf Larsson was selected by Otto Salomon to build a sloyd program in the U.S.; in his book *Elementary Sloyd and Whittling*, he described the objectives of sloyd in a series of questions.

There is often a vague idea of the educational value of manual training. To make this clear, the following questions should be satisfactorily answered by supervisors:

First: Are the child's positions and movements while working likely to be injurious or beneficial to his physical development?

Second: Is he doing his own thinking, unprompted and uninterrupted by the teacher?

Third: Is his work so carried on that self-respect is developed rather than vanity?

Fourth: Is he learning to recognize and to love excellence of workmanship, as shown by becoming more and more critical of himself and his own achievements?

Fifth: Is he learning to recognize good form and to avoid unsuitable decoration?

Sixth: Is he getting some training in good citizenship by working with others?

Seventh: Does the finished product represent the child's own effort, and is the workmanship good, or was the problem too difficult?

In educational sloyd, as adopted from Diesterweg's principles, instruction was to proceed from the known to the unknown, from the easy to the more difficult, from the simple to the complex, and from the concrete to the abstract.

With these principles in mind, projects were designed so that the child's work, intelligence, and skill would proceed accordingly, with one caveat. In accordance with Froebel's philosophy, the interest of the child must always be considered. Larsson warned that "Although the models and the directions here outlined have been planned with great care, it must be understood that they are not recommended as a fixed and unalterable plan of work. Teachers should always change the methods and models in the interest of general improvement or adapt them for special needs."

Educational sloyd was introduced to the U.S. through the Philadelphia Centennial Exposition in 1876. Many of those who promoted kindergarten also became advocates of manual training in the same time frame. While educational sloyd faced competition from the Russian system of manual arts training in the U.S., most of the manual arts programs from the 1880s onward were at least a part of what Froebel had started through his invention of kindergarten.

GIFT 1

[The Ball]

MATERIALS
- 2 x 4 scraps

TOOLS
- Miter box
- Fine-toothed backsaw
- C clamp
- Stop block
- Ruler
- Pencil
- Compass
- Combination square
- Carving knife
- Sandpaper, if desired

The ball was the first of the gifts that Froebel made for the educational play of children. A hard wooden ball chased by a child across the floor, or a fuzzy ball attached to a string and dangled to entertain and teach a child while still on his or her mother's lap, was what Froebel intended as his first gift. Today, balls are commonplace, and can be purchased wherever toys are sold, but there is still a special spirit in the things we have made ourselves. For Froebel, the shape of the ball was one of the essential building blocks of nature, and symbolic of the wholeness of the universe and the holiness of the child. But what would a child learn from play with a ball? How about coordination of hand and eye? How about gravity? How about the density, hardness, and weight of the material? How about something of the very essence of life?

A box of six fuzzy crocheted balls in primary and secondary colors (red, blue, yellow, orange, purple, and green) can be presented in a box as Froebel's first gift.

Making a Miter Box

A simple miter box is the easiest way to make square cuts with a handsaw; during Froebel's lifetime, the use of a backsaw and miter box would have been the best way to cut small blocks of wood and make boxes. Unfortunately, today's mass-produced miter boxes have some deficiencies, and it is best to make your own to ensure that each cut is true. When building the miter box, cut your parts with particular attention to each cut being marked square and cut on the line. Then, use a square to see that you have been successful. If not, cut again. Cutting with a handsaw takes practice and you may not get perfect results from your first cut. By building your miter box in carefully prescribed steps, you can make certain that every cut will be square and everything you make with it will be square also.

MATERIALS
- 1½-in. #6 woodscrews, 10
- Wood, see parts list
- Glue

TOOLS
- Drill or screwdriver
- Square
- Masking tape

PARTS LIST

Number	Part Name	Dimensions	Material
1	Base	¾ x 4½ x 16 in.	White pine
1	Front left	¾ x 4½ x 10 in.	White pine
1	Front right	¾ x 4½ x 6 in.	White pine
1	Rear left	¾ x 4 x 10 in.	White pine
1	Rear right	¾ x 4 x 6 in.	White pine

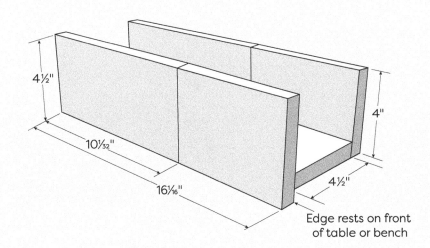

4½"

10¹⁄₃₂"

16¹⁄₁₆"

4"

4½"

Edge rests on front of table or bench

Use a screw to attach the first piece of the front fence to the base board. Note that I've positioned the board so that a portion of it extends below the base. This will either allow the miter box to be clamped in a vise or rest firmly against the edge of the workbench while you cut.

Use a square to make certain that the end of the front fence is square to the base before adding a second screw.

Use a square to align the back fence on the base. I have cut the back fence so that its height will equal the front, with the bottom edge flush with the underside of the base.

To make screwing on this piece easier, apply a bead of glue where the parts join. Tape the piece in position while the glue sets long enough (15 to 20 minutes) so that the piece will not move as screws are driven in.

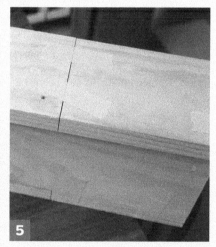

Finally, glue and tape the additional parts on the front and back of the miter box. Leave a thin gap between the parts so that your saw blade will pass through. This will eliminate the need to make a full cut of your own and will increase the accuracy of each cut when you are making blocks or boxes.

Making Gift 1

Start with a Square Block

Use your miter box to cut square blocks first. I use a cutoff piece of 2 x 4 lumber such as you would find thrown away at construction sites; from a small number of scraps, you can make lots of square blocks. This same technique can be applied in later chapters, though other techniques for making blocks more easily with power tools will be shown.

The following technique is appealing to me as I know it to be the one most likely for Friedrich Froebel to have used in the middle of the 19th century. With a bit of practice and a sharp saw, it will work just as well today. You can use any type of saw, but a backsaw with a fine tooth will cut better blocks, and the back on the saw keeps it from cutting too deeply into the base of the miter box. You will need to start with a square end in your 2 x 4

stock. If it is not square, put it in the miter box and cut off a short piece of the end. Then use a stop block and clamp to control the length of your first cut. The stop block should be set at a distance from the saw cut that is equal to the thickness of the stock (approximately 1½ inches) (see **photo 1-1**).

Rotate the piece of wood cut from the length of 2 x 4 and nest it tightly against the stop block. Then use the backsaw to cut through (see **photo 1-2**). Using this technique, you will be able to cut a second block from the original cutoff, so it takes three cuts to make two blocks.

Mark a Circle

Mark the face of each block from corner to corner to find the center, and then use a compass to mark a circle on each face of the

Photo 1-1. Use a miter box and backsaw with a stop block to make the first cut.

Photo 1-2. Rotate the cutoff stock, slide it into position, and use the backsaw to finish cutting the cube shape.

Froebel's Sphere

Froebel believed that the sphere was one of the foundational shapes in the universe. If you look at the sun, the earth, the moon, or another planet, it's a sphere that you see. If you mix soap and water to make bubbles, near-perfect spheres are formed. Many fruiting bodies from the world of plants are spherical in shape. Balls for gift 1 were made from a variety of materials. They can be felted from soft wool or crocheted from yarn. Many young women at the time (and as some are today) were skilled in making crocheted goods. We also know that Froebel

was a skilled whittler, and as a teen had spent time as a forester's apprentice in the Thuringian Forest of central Germany, where he would have become quite familiar with the work of forest craftsmen. His friend the countess Bertha von Marenholtz-Bülow told of him giving her small and lovely carved objects. As a woodworker, myself, I focus here on carving a ball from wood, but there is no reason a skilled parent or grandparent would not want to try a hand at all three methods. Simply do an Internet search for "crocheting a ball" or "felting a ball" to get started.

block. With the tip of the compass placed exactly at center and the distance between tips set at ¾-inch, a perfect circle will be formed on each face that touches each edge (see **photos 1-3** and **1-4**). Use a 45° angle square and pencil to mark a line tangent to

the circle at each corner. Connect the ends of those lines with additional lines across each face, forming a small square on the face of each side. These lines are important guides as you carve material away to form a ball (see **photo 1-5**).

Photo 1-3. Use a compass to mark a circle on each side. You will need to carefully mark the center of each side first. I use a ruler and mark from corner to corner in each direction. Where the lines cross is the place to center the compass for marking the circle.

Photo 1-4. With all the lines drawn from corner to corner on each side and the circles scribed, your cube will look like this.

Photo 1-5. Use a square to mark your first cut lines. Use a combination square at 45° to mark a line just touching the circumference of the circle at each corner, and then use the 90° square to mark between those lines on each side.

Whittle the Sphere

I always begin my whittling doing the hardest part first: cutting across the end grain. Don't try to remove all the stock at once. Thin slices made with the least effort will give the best results (see **photo 1-6**). Continue carving down to the line on each face, carving the end grain first (see **photo 1-7**).

After the ends are cut to shape, tackle the long grain corners, again cutting down to the marked line (see **photo 1-8**). Cutting a number of thin slices will give the best results and you will have to be particularly watchful of the direction of wood grain, as a deep cut can follow the grain deeper into the wood and remove too much stock. After the corners are cut, your block will look like a polygon (see **photo 1-9**).

Cut between the small squares on each face to form small triangles, and you will have a polygon shape that Leonardo da Vinci illustrated in the 15th century (see **photo 1-10**).

At this point, you can choose one of two strategies, each leading to a ball.

Photo 1-6. Make a series of cuts on each corner, deliberately stopping short of your thumb. Less experienced carvers can cover their thumbs with tape to prevent injury.

Photo 1-7. Continue to cut along each corner. I cut across the end grain parts first.

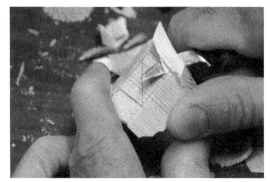

Photo 1-8. When the end grain cuts have been made, proceed to cut along the remaining corners of the block.

Photo 1-9. Your initial polygon will look like this.

Photo 1-10. Draw additional lines forming triangles around the pointy corners that remain. The triangles will form additional squares equal to those drawn on the original sides.

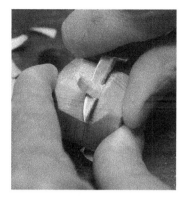

Photo 1-11. You can also begin more intuitively by gradually carving each side to a more circular form.

Photo 1-12. Using a mathematical approach, you can continue marking smaller and smaller squares and triangles as you continue carving.

Photo 1-13. Keep whittling down the corners, one by one. You will eventually produce a near-spherical shape.

Photo 1-14. As you proceed, use your fingers to discern high points. Wherever you feel a large bump, whittle it down. In this way, a sphere will gradually come from your efforts.

Photo 1-15. You can sand the sphere at this point if you like, to further develop its spherical form. My preference is to leave evidence of the knife work.

Simply begin making slicing cuts around the circumference in each plane as shown (see **photo 1-11**), or you can follow a more mathematical approach and mark additional small squares for removal with the knife (see **photo 1-12**). Through a series of small cuts, being very careful to observe the direction of grain, you will gradually arrive at what will be recognized as a ball (see **photo 1-13**). Rotate the ball between your fingers and thumb, and you will find high spots requiring a slice or two more (see **photo 1-14**). It may not be absolutely perfect, but I refuse to sand it perfectly round. I prefer to see all the carefully made knife cuts as evidence that I made it myself (see **photo 1-15**).

Making the Gift 1 Box

PARTS LIST *for the* **GIFT 1 NAILED BOX**

Number	Part Name	Dimensions	Material
2	Low sides	⅜ x 2 x 3¼ in.	White pine*
2	High sides	¼ x 2¼ x 6 in.	White pine*
1	Bottom	⅛ x 3¾ x 6 in.	Baltic birch plywood
1	Lid	⅛ x 3¹⁵⁄₃₂ x 6½ in.	Baltic birch plywood

*or other softwood

MATERIALS

- Wood,
  see parts list
- ⅝-in. #19 nails, 18
- Shellac or
  clear Danish oil,
  if desired
- Glue

TOOLS

- Miter box
- Stop block
- C clamps
- Handsaw
- Shooting board
- Handplane
- Knife
- ⅛-in. chisel
- Hammer
- Sanding block
- Steel stamp set
  and ballpoint pen,
  or pyrography
  equipment

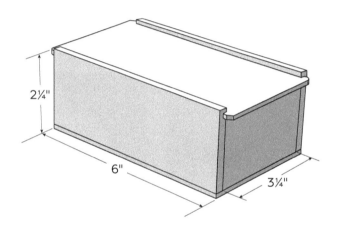

PARTS LIST *for the* **GIFT 1 FINGER-JOINTED BOX**

Number	Part Name	Dimensions	Material
2	Ends	⁵⁄₁₆ x 2¹⁄₁₆ x 3¾ in.	Basswood*
2	Sides	⁵⁄₁₆ x 2½ x 6 in.	Basswood*
1	Lid	⁵⁄₁₆ x 3⅜ x 6 in.	Basswood*
1	Bottom	⅛ x 3¾ x 6 in.	Baltic birch plywood

*or other softwood

Gather the Stock

I have presented here a simple nailed-together construction method for the box. If you'd like to make a finger-jointed box, see gift 3 for instructions and use the parts list shown here. The box holds six balls, whether they are felted, crocheted, or made from wood. To make a box to hold gift 1, use a miter box (as shown on page 22) to cut parts to length (see **photo 1-16**). For this box, use ⅜-inch-thick white pine stock for the low sides and ¼-inch white pine for the high sides. The idea with using the thicker stock for the ends is that it gives additional room for nails to enter

the wood without splitting. Use a stop block clamped in place on the miter box to control the lengths of the parts, so that each set of sides will be equal.

I use a shooting board and handplane to square the ends of the stock after sawing (see **photo 1-17**). To create a shooting board, see the sidebar on page 30. To cut the grooves for the sliding lid to fit, first cut the lid slightly oversize in width and length, referring to the drawing on page 28. It does not need to be cut to perfect size because the fit will be fine-tuned after the box is assembled.

Photo 1-16. Use a miter box to cut box parts to length.

Photo 1-17. Square the ends of the stock after sawing.

Making a Shooting Board

The shooting board is a simple device that craftsmen use to square handsawn stock with a handplane. To make one, simply layer ¼-inch plywood on a thicker base. The ¼-inch plywood holds the stock to be planed at a higher elevation above the sole of the plane, so that the plane's sharp blade can take a thin slice. It works for either end grain or long grain, and a stop is used to hold the stock square to the action of the plane.

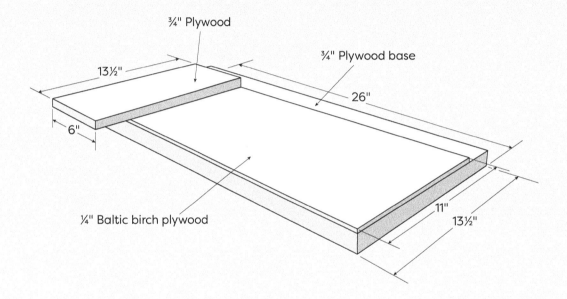

¾" Plywood

¾" Plywood base

13½"

26"

6"

¼" Baltic birch plywood

11"

13½"

Cut the Lid Groove

Lay a piece of 2-inch-wide stock on top of the 2¼-inch sides and clamp it down tight, with the bottom edges aligned. Then, use a sharp knife to score a groove along the edge of the 2-inch stock (see **photo 1-18**). Next, with a piece of ⅛-inch stock held in place to serve as a guide, score another line offset from the first (see **photo 1-19**). I make several shallow cuts to see that it goes deep enough. This process works best with softwoods like white pine. Use a ⅛-inch chisel to cut along the groove

to a depth of almost ⅛ inch (see **photo 1-20**). It is important that this groove be uniform in depth from one end to the other on both the front and back. If you are like most folks (you are), you will get better at this operation with practice, and selecting straight-grained material will be an asset.

Check the fit by sliding the lid through the groove on both front and back (see **photo 1-21**). It should rest evenly at the same depth at each end.

Photo 1-18. Score a groove along the edge of the 2-inch stock.

Photo 1-19. Score another line offset from the first using a piece of ⅛-inch stock as a guide.

Photo 1-20. Use a ⅛-inch chisel to cut the groove to ⅛-inch deep.

Photo 1-21. Check the fit of the lid in the groove.

Assemble the Box

To assemble the box, get your nails started and placed uniformly on the high sides (see **photo 1-22**). Careful spacing is a sign of good craftsmanship. Be sure to leave space at the top for the lid to slide. Spread a layer of glue on each end's edge as you prepare to nail the box together (see **photo 1-23**). Then, with the higher sides carefully aligned at the bottom of the box and short ends, drive the nails into place (see **photo 1-24**).

Cut the ⅛-inch-thick bottom to fit, apply glue to the edges, and drive nails into the end pieces (see **photo 1-25**). Glue alone will be sufficient to hold the bottom to the high sides.

Photo 1-22. Start the nails uniformly on the high sides.

Photo 1-23. Apply glue on each end's edge.

Photo 1-24. Drive the nails into place.

Photo 1-25. Drive nails into the end pieces.

After cutting the ⅛-inch Baltic birch plywood lid roughly to fit, use the shooting board to fine-tune it so that it slides smoothly in the grooves (see **photo 1-26**).

Gently round the ends of the lid and use a sanding block to make all the corners of the box smooth (see **photo 1-27**). Then, if desired, finish the blocks and box with shellac or clear Danish oil. To provide a number on each gift, I use a steel stamp set, then color in the impression with a ballpoint pen. You could also use woodburning equipment, pencil, or pen.

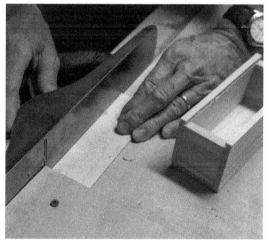

Photo 1-26. Fit the lid.

Photo 1-27. Sand the box corners smooth.

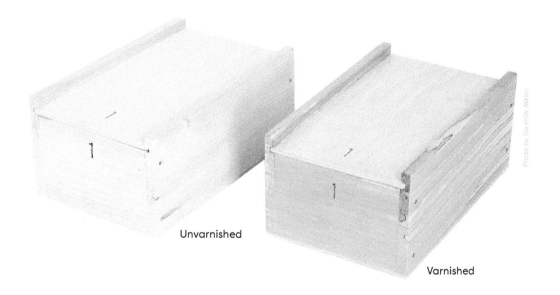

Unvarnished

Varnished

GIFT 2

[Cube, Cylinder, and Sphere]

MATERIALS

- Wood, see parts list
- Thin plywood or thick paper, ⅛ x 1¾ x 1¾ in.

TOOLS

- Miter box
- Saw
- Pencil
- Ruler
- Lathe
- Spindle gouge
- Calipers
- Parting tool
- Skew chisel
- Compass
- Scroll saw or coping saw, or scissors

Friedrich Froebel's second gift became a symbol of his own life. If you were to go to Froebel's gravesite in Thuringia, Germany, you would find his grave marked by gift 2: a sphere, a cylinder, and a cube, neatly stacked just as children might play with this gift, although the marker is made of granite instead of wood, and in much greater scale than those made for children's growth and amusement.

Froebel understood his second gift as building upon the play experience of the child with gift 1. While the sphere of gift 1 might be soft and yielding if made with yarn or felt, gift 2 would be hard and unyielding; this expanded the child's understanding of geometry in new ways. The sphere, cylinder, and cube were not just to hold or look

at, but demanded by their very nature to be put in motion. A sphere can roll any which way, but a cylinder rolls only along a certain orientation back or forth, but not to the side. A cube, on the other hand, is solid and immovable in comparison.

As kindergarten became an international movement focused just on the year before first grade, rather than what Froebel intended—a means of engaging toddlers in playful exploration—Froebel devised all kinds of new ways for older children to use gift 2 (see **figure 2-1**). Tightly wound strings manipulated by a stick set the suspended sphere, cylinder, and cube in motion so that each would take on the appearance of the other. For instance, a spinning sphere is always spherical in shape, but a spinning cube can

take on the appearance of a cylinder, and a spinning cylinder, if suspended at just the right angle, can look like a sphere (see **figure 2-2**). Instructions will be given here to create these spinning shapes—but if you can imagine a toddler playing on the floor with a ball that rolls with a mind of its own, and a cylinder that rolls only in prescribed ways, and a cube planted solidly on the floor, you realize that these shapes need no extra magic than that with which they are endowed.

Frank Lloyd Wright's mother, who visited a kindergarten exhibit at the Philadelphia Centennial Exposition in 1876, gave him a set of Froebel's gift 2. The famous architect attributed his becoming an architect to his play with Froebel's blocks.

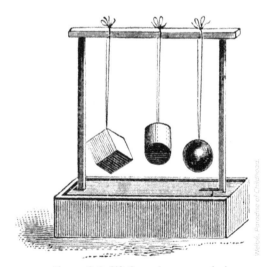

Figure 2-1. Gift 2 can be suspended.

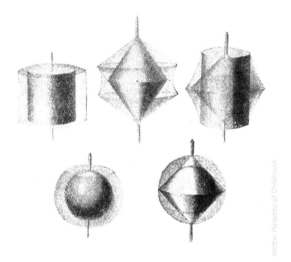

Figure 2-2. The parts of gift 2 can be rotated.

Gifts as Transitions

Friedrich Froebel believed that what he called "self-activity" was a child's most important teacher—that by giving children gifts inspiring investigation into the properties of the universe, they would be launched into a lifetime of investigation and direct observation. Froebel also devised songs and teacher-led play to invite the student to observe particular qualities inherent in the gifts, stimulating examination of similarities and differences between shapes. He designed his gifts to lead one into the other in a natural progression through which the child's intelligence and character would be formed. Not only is gift 2 transformational; it also serves as a transition from gift 1, the sphere, to what some have called his building gifts, 3, 4, 5, 5B, and 6, that each consist of a set of blocks that fit neatly within special boxes.

Froebel's Foresting Experience

During Froebel's lifetime, itinerant craftsmen were commonplace in the forests throughout Europe, where they harvested materials for fabricating small furniture. They would cut and split logs for making lumber and turn legs on portable spring pole lathes for stools, chairs, and tables. In his early life, Froebel apprenticed as a forester's assistant in the Thuringian Forest; as such, he would have been well-acquainted with the crafts practiced by woodsmen, and perhaps even tried his hand at their crafts.

Making Gift 2

PARTS LIST *for* GIFT 2

	Number	Part Name	Dimensions	Material
⬤	1	Sphere	1½ x 1½ x 1½ in.	White pine or basswood
⬭	1	Cylinder	1½ x 1½ x 1½ in.	White pine or basswood
⬚	1	Cube	1⅝ x 1⅝ x 1⅝ in.	White pine or basswood

If you can whittle a ball from a cube of wood as we did in the last chapter, the cylinder and cube will be easy for you. Just as you carved a sphere, the cylinder can be whittled with a knife and with far less difficulty. However, the lathe is the modern craftsman's tool of choice for making spheres and cylinders. In fact, as kindergarten became an international movement, companies like Milton Bradley in the U.S. used lathes to make gift 2 in large quantities to meet the growing need.

Prepare to Turn

To make a turned cylinder and sphere, start with a piece of wood with plenty of excess length: long enough to have space at each end of each object to give full range of motion to the tools as they shape the spinning wood. Cut the cube from the stock using a miter box before proceeding.

Mark the location of the center at each end (see **photo 2-1**). It is important to be precise. If the wood is off-center, it will still turn round

Photo 2-1. Use a straight ruler and mark carefully from corner to corner in each direction to find the center of the stock on the ends.

Photo 2-2. Mount the stock between centers on the lathe and turn it to a cylinder.

given enough time, but this will require greater effort and cause greater vibration, and you'll end up with a smaller cylinder and sphere than you might intend. Lines drawn between corners of square stock will easily mark center.

Turn the Cylinder

Mount the stock between centers on the lathe and use a gouge to rough out the cylindrical shape (see **photo 2-2**). When you have formed a cylinder perfectly smooth and round from one end to the other, use a caliper to determine the diameter (see **photo 2-3**). Then, use the caliper to mark the lengths of the cylinder and sphere directly on the stock, leaving some space between so that the tools can move around the shape of the sphere (see **photo 2-4**). Use a parting tool to begin defining the length of the cylinder, but leave enough stock at the center so that the whole length still has strength for the next step (see **photo 2-5**). At this point, except for cutting it to final length, the cylinder is complete and you can turn your attention to the sphere.

Shape the Sphere

Mark a centerline between the two ends of the stock intended to become the sphere and then begin forming 45° flats on each end, using the centerline to help observe that what you do to one end is also done to the other (see **photo 2-6**).

Use a skew chisel to begin rounding the sphere on both ends (see **photo 2-7**). This is a gradual process, and I am careful not to work

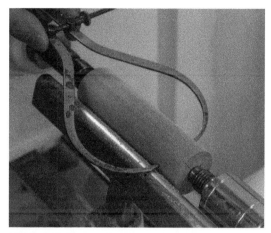

Photo 2-3. Use a caliper to determine the diameter of the turned cylinder.

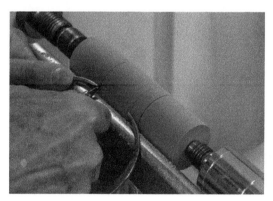

Photo 2-4. Use the caliper and pencil or pen to mark the wood with the lengths of the sphere and cylinder.

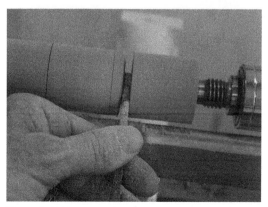

Photo 2-5. Use a parting tool to cut partway in to form the cylinder.

too much with the chisel at the center. As long as I've not worn away the pencil line at the center of the sphere, I know that I've not reduced its diameter.

Complete the Gift

I use a homemade gauge to help assess the final shape (see **photo 2-8**). To make the guide, use a compass to scribe an arc on thin plywood or thick paper, with the radius equal to half the diameter of the cylinder. Use a scroll saw or coping saw (or scissors, if using paper) to cut out the shape. Hold it up to the sphere to assess your results. Finally, use a small handsaw to liberate the sphere and cylinder from the balance of the stock and sand the ends smooth.

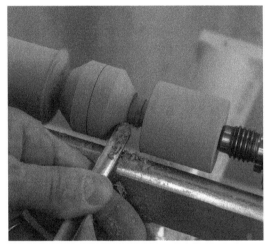

Photo 2-6. Begin to form the sphere by making equal-sized flat facets at each end.

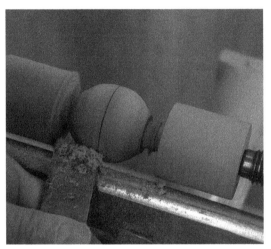

Photo 2-7. Gradually round the flats between the centerline and the ends of the sphere.

Photo 2-8. Check the progress in making the sphere.

Making the Gift 2 Box

To make the plain box for gift 2, see the instructions for the gift 1 box on page 28. The dimensions are different, but the construction method is the same.

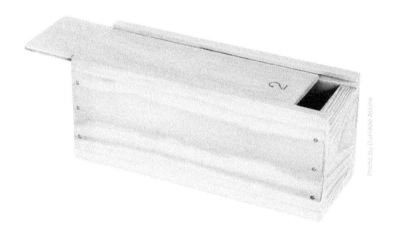

Photo by Danielle Atkins

PARTS LIST *for* GIFT 2 BOX

Number	Part Name	Dimensions	Material
2	Low sides	⅜ x 2 x 1¾ in.	White pine*
2	High sides	¼ x 2¼ x 6 in.	White pine*
1	Bottom	¼ x 2¼ x 6 in.	White pine*
1	Lid	⅛ x 1³¹⁄₃₂ x 6½ in.	Baltic birch plywood

*or other softwood

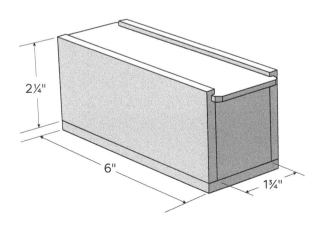

2¼"

6"

1¾"

Making the Gift 2 Combined Box Stand

There are two ways to put Froebel's forms from gift 2 in motion. One is to drill a hole clear through the shapes for a stick to fit. That is a major challenge for most craftsmen. For instance, drilling a hole from one corner of a cube to another allows the drill bit numerous opportunities to wander off course and emerge in the wrong place on the other side. Milton Bradley and

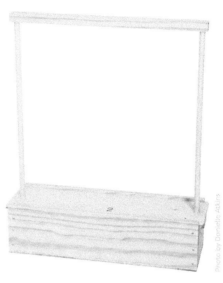

others managed to devise a technique for drilling accurately all the way through; however, this still remains out of reach for most home craftsmen. The easiest way to set Froebel's gift 2 in motion is to suspend the objects on loops of string using small screw eyes to attach the string to a corner of the object.

One option is to create a box with a built-in stand in the lid for spinning the shapes. The instructions are much the same as the box for gift 1 (see page 28), with a few differences. To make a box that supports poles for spinning the shapes, you will need to drill holes in the ends centered in the box ends and matching holes through the sliding lid (see **photo 2-9**). In addition, cuts must be made for storing the poles

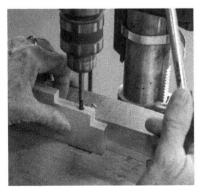

when the set is put away. These cuts in the end pieces should be ½-inch deep by ⅝-inch long; with the end pieces glued in place, the cuts form a recess for the support apparatus to be stored.

Photo 2-9. Drill holes in the ends to support the dowel rods.

MATERIALS

- Wood, see parts list
- ⅝-in. #19 nails, 18
- Small eye screws, 3
- 16-in. length of string
- Shellac or clear Danish oil, if desired

TOOLS

- Miter box
- Saw
- Drill and bit
- Sanding block
- Hammer
- Steel stamp set and ballpoint pen, or pyrography equipment

PARTS LIST *for* GIFT 2 COMBINED BOX STAND

Number	Part Name	Dimensions	Material
2	Low sides	½ x 2 x 2½ in.	White pine*
2	High sides	¼ x 2¼ x 9 in.	White pine*
1	Bottom	⅛ x 3 x 9 in.	Baltic birch plywood
1	Lid	⅛ x 2²³⁄₃₂ x 9⅜ in.	Baltic birch plywood
2	End caps	⅛ x 1¼ x ¾ in.	White pine*
2	Support dowels	¼ x 9 in.	Hardwood
1	Horizontal beam	⅜ x ½ x 9 in.	White pine*

*or other softwood

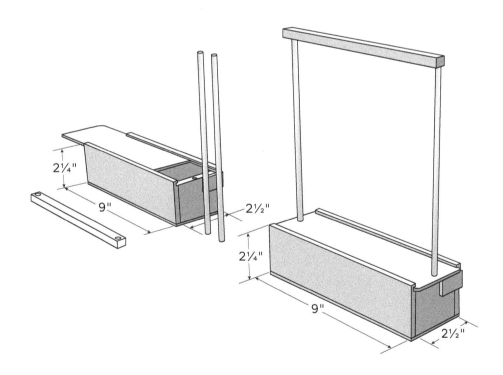

Making the Gift 2 Stand

A simpler variation to put gift 2 in motion is to build a stand-alone stand, paired with the plain box for storage. Simply cut the base to size from ¾-inch stock that is 3½ x 9½ inches; drill holes for the dowels in both the base and the horizontal beam the same distance apart; screw the small eye screws into the shapes; and tie a string loop through the eye screws.

Photo by Danielle Atkins

MATERIALS
- Wood, see parts list
- Small eye screws, 3
- 16-in. length of string

TOOLS
- Miter box
- Saw
- Drill and bit
- Sanding block

PARTS LIST *for the* GIFT 2 STAND

Number	Part Name	Dimensions	Material
1	Base	¾ x 3½ x 9½ in.	White pine*
2	Support dowels	¼ x 9 in.	Hardwood
1	Horizontal beam	⅜ x ½ x 9 in.	White pine*

*or other softwood

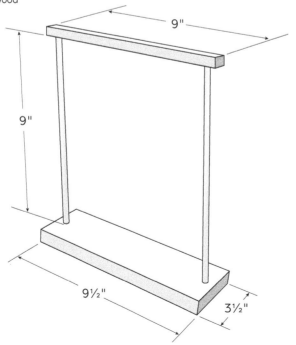

9"

9"

9½"

3½"

GIFT 3

[Cube Divided into Cubes]

MATERIALS
- Wood, see parts list
- Masking tape, optional

TOOLS
- Tablesaw with blade
- Sled
- Stop block
- Pencil with eraser

Gift 3 is a set of eight small cubes in a box also shaped like a cube; it is what many consider the first of Froebel's "building or construction" gifts. Gifts 3, 4, 5, 5B, and 6 each contain sets of blocks for building. Blocks kept in such an orderly fashion would be almost unheard of in jumbled American toy chests; however, this gift is not just for play, but was developed with serious intent. The construction gifts were meant to be used one set after another in progression as the child grew in dexterity, knowledge, and imagination. We know Froebel used building blocks in his first school, long before he invented kindergarten and made his mark on worldwide education.

Each of the gifts can be used in three different ways, and the small cubes in gift number 3 are a great example. They can be used in counting; in understanding geometric form, with the larger cube being formed by eight smaller ones; and can be arranged into shapes. One manner of arranging shapes is to represent objects within the child's home and family; these are called "forms of life." For instance, removing two smaller cubes forms the shape of grandfather's chair (see **photo 3-1**). In that way, gift 3 is used to describe and explore the child's relationships with home, community, and family. Another way to arrange the cubes is to express harmony and symmetry; these are called "forms of beauty." It was important to Froebel's idea of education that children should explore a relationship with beauty (see **photo 3-2**). A third way to arrange the gifts is "forms of knowledge." These forms are meant to help the child explore math and science by sorting and ordering the pieces. Between the three types of forms, children can find innumerable ways to creatively express themselves (see sidebar on page 50).

One of the special features of gifts 3 through 6 is that all the blocks stacked together form a cube (see **photo 3-3**); the gift can be neatly repackaged by placing the box over the cube (see **photo 3-4**) and sliding the box and its contents onto the lid (see **photo 3-5**). Turn the box right side up and the gift is ready to put away for the next lesson.

Photo 3-1. Gift number 3 consists of eight 1-inch cubes. Six blocks arranged in this "form of life" represent grandfather's chair.

Photo 3-2. In addition to representational shapes, "forms of beauty" arranged on a flat surface introduce the child to 2D design.

Historically Speaking:
Froebel's Blocks

As described in *Paradise of Childhood* and other books about the life of Froebel, during the summer of 1817, Froebel and his associate Middendorf "lived in a wretched little hut with neither door, flooring or stove, while Froebel was building a schoolhouse" at Keilhau in the mountains of the Thuringian Forest. His small quarters had previously served as a hen house. In July, one of his friends, Langenthal, stopped to visit on his way to Silesia, where he had become engaged as a tutor to nobility. He was taking his younger brother with him. When he arrived, Froebel's students were lying on the floor at play with wooden blocks that Froebel had designed and made. The students were building forts and castles, and Langenthal's brother excitedly joined the play. He built an elaborate Gothic cathedral, and Langenthal decided it would be wrong to tear his brother from the play. He decided then and there that he and his brother would stay and become part of Froebel's school. We know from this story that from Froebel's earliest days as an educator, play with blocks was an important part of Froebel's scheme for learning.

Photo 3-3. Stack the blocks together to form a cube.

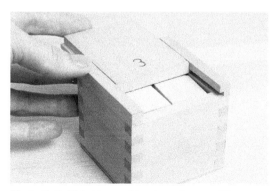

Photo 3-5. Slide the upside-down box and its contents off the table and onto the lid, using it to keep the blocks inside. Then flip the box and its contents over and slide the lid in place. Gift 3 will be safely put away until the next day's play.

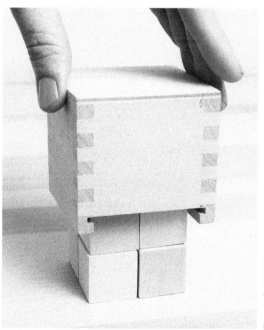

Photo 3-4. Place the box over the cube.

GIFT 3—THINGS YOU CAN MAKE

FORMS OF LIFE

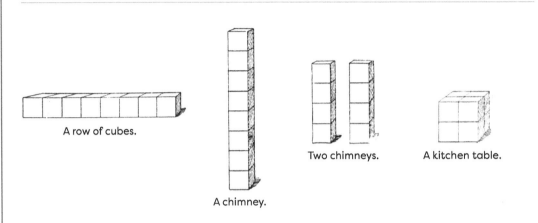

A row of cubes.

A chimney.

Two chimneys.

A kitchen table.

FORMS OF KNOWLEDGE

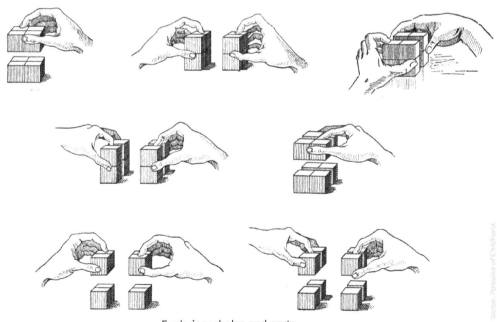

Exploring wholes and parts.

FORMS OF BEAUTY

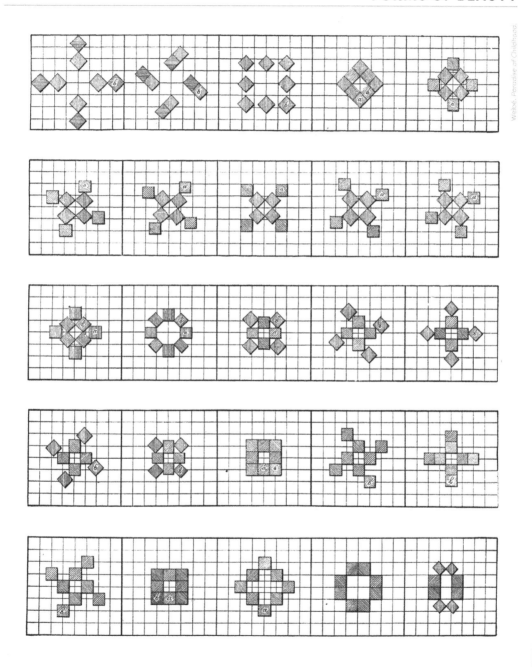

Welte, *Paradise of Childhood*.

Making Gift 3

PARTS LIST *for* GIFT 3

	Number	Part Name	Dimensions	Material
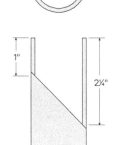	8	Cubes	1 x 1 x 1 in.	Basswood*

*or other medium-density hardwood

Cut the Stock to Dimension

Gift 3's 1-inch cubes can be cut using a miter box and saw. For those of you with wood shops and power tools in need of projects, these blocks and the boxes to hold them can be quickly made in quantities sufficient for a small preschool.

My secret for making lots and lots of blocks and the boxes necessary to hold them is the tablesaw sled. Equipped with a stop block, it carries the wood safely through the cut, keeping it under exacting control and your fingers at a safe distance. The use of the stop block will assure that each block is the same length. It is also useful for making a box, or a dozen boxes, because it will make certain that each part is squarely cut to the exact length

> ⚠ **WARNING**
>
> Note: According to the United States Consumer Product Safety Commission, the small parts regulation "prevents deaths and injuries to children under three from choking on, inhaling, or swallowing small objects they may 'mouth.' It bans toys and other articles that are intended for use by children under three and that are or have small parts, or that produce small parts when broken." To satisfy this regulation, any toys or parts of toys must not be able to fit "completely into a specially designed test cylinder 2.25 inches long by 1.25 inches wide that approximates the size of the fully expanded throat of a child under three years old" (see figure at right). A cube measuring 1 inch (gift 3) on each side or a tile ½ x 1 x 2 inches (gift 4) fits this standard; as we begin making the blocks on gifts 5, 5B, 6, and 7, it should be noted that the smaller size blocks can present a choking hazard and should be used only by older children.

Photo 3-6. Plane or saw wood to a 1-inch thickness and then rip it into 1-inch-wide strips for making blocks.

required. You can make these same cuts using a standard miter guide on a tablesaw, but with less accuracy, and with a slightly greater amount of risk, as the cut-off stock is left near the blade instead of being pulled back along with the sled for safe removal.

To begin making the blocks, use the tablesaw to rip the stock to dimension. You can use standard 2 x 4s to get full 1-inch stock, or saw and plane hardwood stock to dimension. In **photo 3-6** I am sawing basswood that I first planed to a thickness of 1 inch.

Cut the Blocks

After rip-sawing the stock to length, use the tablesaw, sled, and stop block to cut the blocks

to uniform size. Use the eraser end of a pencil to hold the block in position as you make the cut (see **photo 3-7**). The eraser end of the pencil is also useful for moving the cut block out of the way and to the side in preparation for the next cut. And having the pencil in hand keeps you from being tempted to reach in toward the spinning blade. Carefully sand each block and apply a finish if desired.

Tip: If you want to make many more blocks than just for your own use, try taping several pieces of stock together with masking tape, so that they can be cut and handled at the same time.

Photo 3-7. Use the cross-cut sled on the tablesaw to cut the blocks to a 1-inch length. A stop block is clamped to the sled to control the length of the blocks. I use a pencil as a hold-down during the cut to keep the block under complete control. When the sled is pulled back from the cut, the block can be safely removed.

Making the Gift 3 Finger-Jointed Box

I made a box with finger joints for gift 3; the finest examples of kindergarten boxes made by craftsmen in Germany or by Milton Bradley Company during the 19th and early 20th centuries were finger-jointed. This type of box is amazingly strong and long-lasting, and original boxes of blocks from Froebel kindergartens are prized collectables today. However, if you'd like to make a nailed box, I've included a parts list for that option.

MATERIALS
- Wood, see parts list
- Glue
- ⅝-in. #19 nails, 6
- Shellac or clear Danish oil, if desired

TOOLS
- Tablesaw with blade
- Sled
- Stop block
- Pencil with eraser
- Finger joint router table, router, and ¼-in.-diameter spiral router bit; or finger joint tablesaw jig
- Push block
- Glue squeeze bottle
- Pin-nailer or hammer
- Sanding block
- Steel stamp set and ballpoint pen, or pyrography equipment

PARTS LIST *for the* FINGER-JOINTED GIFT 3 BOX

Number	Part Name	Dimensions	Material
2	Low sides	⁵⁄₁₆ x 2¹⁄₁₆ x 2¾ in.	Basswood
2	High sides	⁵⁄₁₆ x 2⅜ x 2¾ in.	Basswood
1	Bottom	⅛ x 2¾ x 2¾ in.	Baltic birch plywood
1	Lid	⁵⁄₁₆ x 2⁵⁄₁₆ x 2¾ in.	Basswood

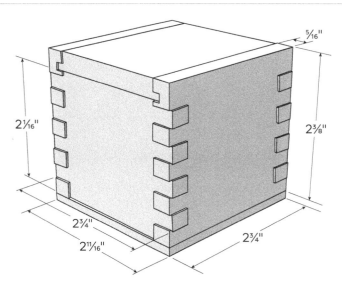

Making a Nailed Box for Gift 3

If you prefer to avoid finger joints, you can create a nailed box for gift 3. Simply follow the instructions for gift 1's box, but use these part dimensions. Note you will need a pin-nailer or hammer, and 16 nails that are 5/8-inch #19.

PARTS LIST *for the* **NAILED GIFT 3 BOX**

Number	Part Name	Dimensions	Material
2	Low sides	3/8 x 2 1/16 x 2 1/16 in.	White pine*
2	High sides	1/4 x 2 5/16 x 2 7/8 in.	White pine*
1	Bottom	1/8 x 2 9/16 x 2 7/8 in.	Baltic birch plywood
1	Lid	1/8 x 2 9/32 x 3 1/4 in.	Baltic birch plywood

*or other softwood

Making a Finger Joint Router Table

I use a shop-made finger joint router table to form finger joints on the box parts. This same operation can be performed with a finger joint jig on the tablesaw, but I've found that the router gives a clean cut and I can leave it set up to make lots of boxes without changing the setting, and without diverting the use of the tablesaw. It is also easy to unclamp and put away when not in use. If you often make finger joints in a variety of sizes, you may want to make sliding tables and fences for more than one bit size. The base, where the router is mounted, can fit more than one size of sliding table.

PARTS LIST *for* **MAKING A FINGER JOINT ROUTER TABLE**

Number	Part Name	Dimensions	Material
1	Base	3/4 x 15 x 22 in.	Plywood or MDF
1	Sliding table	3/4 x 12 x 15 in.	Plywood or MDF
2	Runners	5/8 x 3/4 x 22 in.	Maple
1	Fence	3/4 x 4 1/4 x 15 in.	Maple

MATERIALS

- Wood, see parts list
- #6 1-in. screws, 4
- 1-in. screws sized to fit router base

TOOLS

- Tablesaw with fence, sled, and 3/4-in. dado blade
- Plane
- Pencil or awl
- Drill with 1 3/8-in. drill bit, 1/4-in. drill bit, and countersink
- Fixed base router with 1/4-in. spiral straight cut bit
- 1/4-in. router bit to use as guide pin
- Clamp

Making a Finger Joint Router Table, *continued*

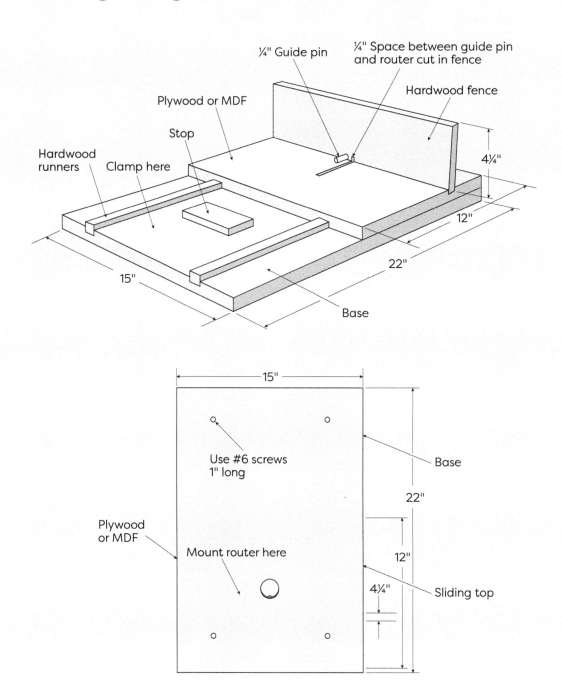

¼" Guide pin

¼" Space between guide pin and router cut in fence

Plywood or MDF

Hardwood fence

Stop

Hardwood runners

Clamp here

4¼"

12"

15"

22"

Base

15"

Use #6 screws 1" long

Base

22"

12"

Plywood or MDF

Mount router here

4¼"

Sliding top

Cut the Base and Sliding Table. Cut your parts to size for these two pieces. Mount a ¾-inch dado blade in the tablesaw with the height set at ⅜-inch. Set the fence 1½ inches from the blade and cut parallel dados along both edges of the plywood stock, halfway through the stock. Complete this for both the top and bottom plywood parts. Cut a dado for the fence to fit in the sliding piece.

Cut the Runners and Fence. Plane the runners and fence to fit. The runners should be an almost-tight fit for smooth sliding; too loose, and they will lose some accuracy. The fence should be planed to snugly fit the dado. When it almost needs to be forced into place, this will hold parts in correct relationship to each other. Cut the fence's length to exactly correspond with the width of the plywood parts.

Mount Router Base and Runners. Mark a centerline for mounting the router base. Use a 1⅜-inch drill bit to drill a hole in the base for the router collet to fit. The router collet should be able to spin freely after mounting. Remove the base plate from the router and position it over the collet hole. Mark the location of the screw holes for mounting the router base to the table base. Drill and countersink screw holes from the top side. Drill and countersink holes for attaching the runners to the base.

Rout the Sliding Base. Clamp the router table base to a workbench corner. Place the fence in the sliding table and gradually raise the router bit. A stop positioned on the base will keep the slot from being lengthened or allowing the bit to be exposed on the back side of the fence.

Fit the Guide Pin. Carefully measure and mark the location for the guide pin. I use the shaft of a ¼-inch router bit as the guide pin. The round shape allows the workpiece to lift on and off the router table easily, and the guide pin can be fitted exactly by simply drilling a ¼-inch hole in the fence and pushing the pin in place. In addition, the round shape of the pin helps to keep small bits of sawdust from getting in the way as you lift the parts into place. To mark the location for the guide pin, measure ⅜-inch in from where the router bit cuts into the fence, mark the location with a sharp awl, and drill the hole with a ¼-inch bit. The guide pin should fit finger-tight within the router cut in the sliding table. The amount of friction you feel inserting it in the slot will be the same as what you will feel as each finger is lifted over the guide pin for the next to be cut; a close, but not forced, fit is best.

Complete Test Cuts. To prepare for the first test cuts, raise the height of the router bit to just barely over the thickness of the stock. Place the test piece snug to the guide pin and make the first cut (see **photos 3-9** through **3-11** for a visual example). Step the workpiece over the guide pin for each subsequent cut. When all cuts have been made, turn the piece over from one face to the other; use it as a spacer to position the next cut. Continue with the cuts on the matching part and test the fit.

Adjust the Fit. If the fingers fit together too tightly, use a mallet to tap lightly on the fence at the right side to narrow the space between the guide pin and router cut. If the fit is too loose, tap lightly on the left. After making the adjustment, cut another test set. When you get a perfect fit, use screws to secure the fence position.

Cut the Box Sides

Use the sled to cut your box sides to size and length, following the dimensions in the parts list (see **photo 3-8**). Again, a stop block clamped to the sled will control the exact length and the eraser end of the pencil will serve to both keep the cut-off part under control, and help to move it out of the way after the cut.

Cut the Finger Joints

When cutting the fingers, you will notice that they stand slightly proud so they can be sanded flush.

With a ¼-inch-diameter spiral router bit in the router, form the fingers on the two high sides first, leaving the short sides for later. Place what will be the bottom edge of the part against the guide pin, and form the first finger. Subsequent fingers are formed by stepping each newly cut finger over the guide pin (see **photo 3-9**). Be careful to leave one

finger extra-wide at the top to allow for the sliding lid to fit. Cut one end and then flip the work piece end-for-end, keeping the bottom edge against the guide pin as you cut fingers on the other side.

When you have cut the fingers on the two high sides, use one piece flipped side-to-side (not end-for-end) over the guide pin. This part will serve as a spacer as you make the first finger cuts on the short sides of the box. Please look carefully at **photo 3-10** to see how the one finished part is used to position the other. When you have routed the first cuts in the short sides, then you can proceed to cut the rest of the fingers on these parts (see **photo 3-11**).

Next, cut the short sides of the box to provide clearance for the lid to slide over. I use the tablesaw to make this cut, and use a shop-made push block to keep my fingers safe from the blade (see **photo 3-12**). For this operation the blade height should be set only

Photo 3-8. Use the sled and stop block on the tablesaw to cut the box sides to the required length.

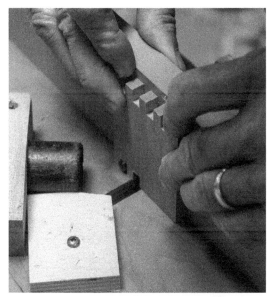

Photo 3-9. Use a finger joint jig to cut the finger joints. This device can be made for either a router or tablesaw. My preferred method is this dedicated finger joint router table described in the sidebar on page 55. Starting with a high side piece, put the edge of the stock against the guide pin, rout a slot between fingers, and then lift it over the guide pin to form the next. Make only four ¼-inch cuts on each end.

Photo 3-10. To begin forming the fingers on the adjoining piece, flip the first piece around so the opposite face is against the body of the jig and one finger is filling the space between the guide and the cut. Make an initial cut on each end of the stock.

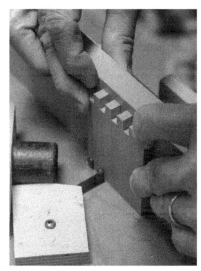

Photo 3-11. Proceed through the rest of the cuts.

Photo 3-12. Trim the height of the short sides on the tablesaw. This is necessary for the lid to slide on and off.

slightly higher than the thickness of the stock. To make the grooves in the box sides for the sliding lid to fit, keep the fence set in the same position and lower the blade height to about ⅛-inch. Again, use the push block to guide the material through the cut (see **photo 3-13**).

Assemble the Box

A trial fit shows the arrangement of parts (see **photo 3-14**).To assemble the boxes, use a small squeeze bottle to apply just a dab of glue in each joint (see **photo 3-15**). A tight-fitting finger joint requires very little glue to form a lasting joint.

Make the Lid

To add a sliding lid made from solid wood, use the tablesaw to cut a small tongue on the edge. First cut the stock to the full width of the opening at the top of the box, plus the depth of the grooves cut on each side piece. Then use a sacrificial fence clamped to the

Photo 3-13. Lower the blade height to ⅛-inch to cut the grooves for the sliding lid to fit in the box high sides.

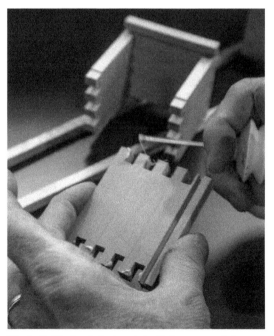

Photo 3-15. Apply just a dab of glue on each finger before final assembly.

Photo 3-14. Test-fit the finger joints.

tablesaw fence so that the blade can be raised to make the cut without damaging the fence. Cut on each side using a ripping blade with a square-topped cut (see **photo 3-16**).

Attach the Bottom

Add a bead of glue along the bottom edge and glue the bottom in place; the bottom is made to fit the finished dimensions of the box, taking into consideration the fingers as sanded flush (see **photo 3-17**). You can

use either a pin-nailer as shown or short brads driven by hand to add additional reinforcement (see **photo 3-18**).

Finish the Box

Carefully sand the edges of the box. Then, if desired, finish the box with shellac or clear Danish oil. To provide a number on each gift, I use a steel stamp set, then color in the impression with a ballpoint pen. You could also use pyrography equipment.

Photo 3-16. Cut the lid to fit the widest point from the groove on one side to the groove on the other, and then form a tongue by making a small tablesaw cut. The stock clamped to the tablesaw fence keeps the blade from touching the fence and also buries the blade to keep the fingers safe.

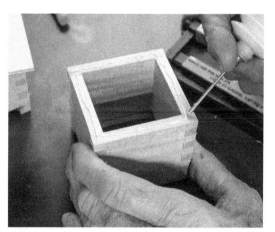

Photo 3-17. Apply a bit of glue to the bottom of the box.

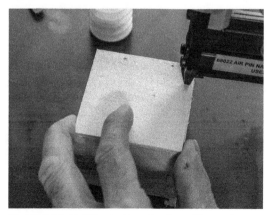

Photo 3-18. Nail the bottom in place. Use a pin-nailer, or hand-driven brads for a lasting fit.

GIFT 4

[Cube Divided into Tiles]

MATERIALS

- Wood, see parts list
- Masking tape, optional

TOOLS

- Tablesaw with blade
- Sled
- Stop block
- Pencil with eraser

Photo 4-1. Use the same technique described on page 53 to cut the rectangular tiles for gift number 4. Eight pieces will be required.

Gift 4, like gift 3, consists of a box filled with eight blocks that form a cube measuring 2 x 2 inches. However, the blocks in gift 3 are cubes, and the blocks in gift 4 are wooden tiles ½ x 1 x 2 inches. The flat tiles offer a different building experience; they are similar to bricks, and thus offer a glimpse of actual construction techniques that can be observed in the real world. Gift 4's pieces also are used to create symmetrical patterns (forms of beauty), but require greater thoughtfulness in their use than the squares of gift 3. Follow the directions starting on page 52 to create gift 3, but make tiles instead of small cubes (see **photo 4-1**). The box for gift 4 is identical to the box for gift 3 (page 54).

PARTS LIST *for* GIFT 4

	Number	Part Name	Dimensions	Material
	8	Tiles	½ x 1 x 2 in.	Basswood*

*or other medium-density hardwood

GIFT 4 – THINGS YOU CAN MAKE

FORMS OF LIFE

The cube.

Part of a floor, or top of a table.

Two large boards.

Four small boards.

Eight building blocks.

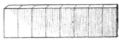
A long garden wall.

A fountain.

Closed garden wall.

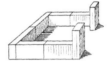
An open garden.

An open garden.

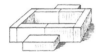
Watering trough.

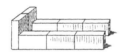
Shooting stand.

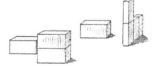
Village.

Triumphal arch.

Merry-go-round.

Large garden settee.

Seat.

Settee.

Sofa.

Two chairs.

FORMS OF BEAUTY

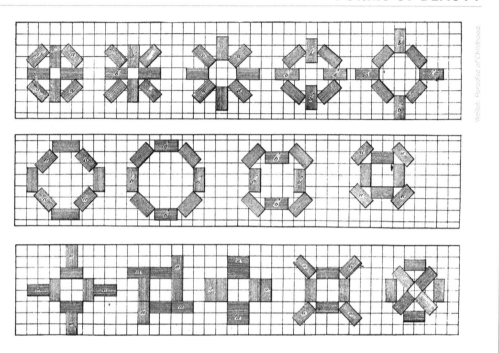

FORMS OF KNOWLEDGE

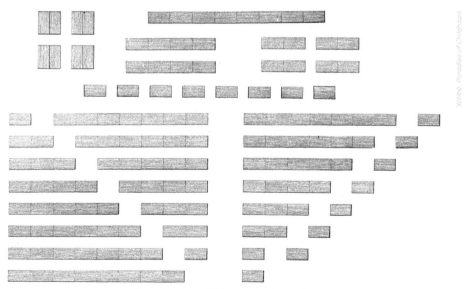

Exercises in addition and subtraction.

GIFT 5

[Cubes, Half-Cubes, and Quarter-Cubes]

MATERIALS

- Wood, see parts list
- Shellac or clear Danish oil, if desired

TOOLS

- Plane
- Tablesaw with sled and blade
- Square
- Push stick
- Stop block
- Pencil with eraser
- Sanding block

Gift 5 is a more complex version of gift 3. Instead of eight small cubes, there are 39 total pieces, including cubes that have been cut in half from corner to corner, and cubes that have been cut into quarters by cutting from corner to corner twice. Arranged in three layers, these blocks form a 3-inch cube. The box is slightly larger to accommodate the increase in pieces. This gift offers a graphic illustration of Froebel's core principles—that learning must move from the known to the unknown, from the easy to the more difficult, from the simple to the complex, and from the concrete to the abstract. The number of blocks in gift 5 adds greatly to the possible designs a child might achieve. The gift also requires greater hand and eye coordination, and greater stacking skill to achieve more complex forms. For children already familiar with the limitations of gifts 3 and 4, gift 5 offers a newly expanded universe commensurate with a new level of development.

GIFT 5—THINGS YOU CAN MAKE

FORMS OF LIFE

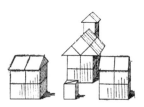

Chapel with hermitage.

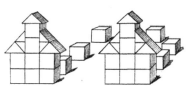

Two garden houses
with rows of trees.

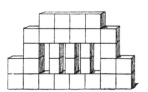

A castle.

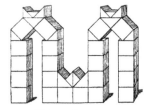

Cloister in ruins.

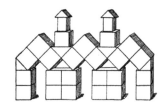

City gate with three entrances.

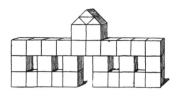

Arsenal.

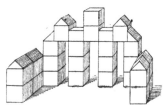

City gate with
two guard-houses.

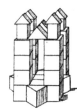

A monument. First row, nine whole and
four half cubes; second to fourth row,
each, four whole cubes; on either side,
two quarter cubes, united to a square
column, and to unite the four columns,
two half cubes.

FORMS OF KNOWLEDGE

A cube.

A cube divided
into three layers.

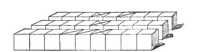

Three rows, showing that the
volume is the same while the
appearance differs.

FORMS OF BEAUTY

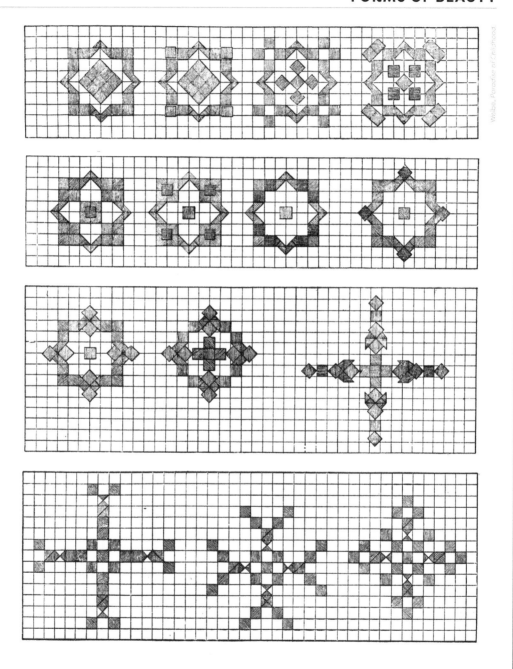

Making Gift 5

PARTS LIST *for* GIFT 5

	Number	Part Name	Dimensions	Material
	21	Whole cubes	1 x 1 x 1 in.	Basswood*
	6	Half cubes	1 x 1 x 1 in. cube divided corner to corner	Basswood*
	12	Quarter cubes	1 x 1 x 1 in. cube divided from corner to corner twice	Basswood*

*or other medium-density hardwood

As with the earlier gifts, Froebel's gift 5 can be made with either power tools or handtools. Power tools simply speed up the process, allowing a single craftsman to make sets for a number of children at the same time, and with greater accuracy. As the sets become more complex, the accuracy of each block becomes more important; many modern craftsmen would have great difficulty making sets with handtools. For crafting this gift, power tools are preferred.

Start the Halved Blocks

Gift 5, in addition to the blocks featured in gift 3, requires blocks that are halved and quartered. These give additional design options, and present greater complexity to the student, allowing growth in both manual dexterity and in development of new forms. Plane material to a 1-inch thickness and then tilt the saw blade to a 45° angle (see **photo 5-1**). The stock must first be cut to a uniform width, so that the angle cut can liberate the

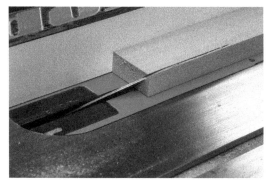

Photo 5-1. Cutting triangular blocks requires the use of a tablesaw. Plane the stock to 1-inch thick. Tilt the blade to 45° and adjust the fence so that the triangle stock is formed on the outside the cut.

Photo 5-2. Form the smaller triangles next by making a ripping cut with the blade back at a 90° angle.

halved stock to the outside of the cut. Have a push stick ready to finish the cut. I prefer to work in wood at least 2 feet long for it to be safely controlled through the cut.

Start the Quartered Blocks

Next, cut the stock for making the quartered cubes. Return the blade angle to 90°. Turn the remaining stock over and adjust the width of the cut so that the angled piece will be 1³⁄₁₆-inches wide along its base (see **photo 5-2**). Use a push stick to finish the cut. Cut the stock that remains into material 1-inch square for making cube blocks.

Cut Blocks to Length

Cut the cube-shaped blocks and the angled half- and quarter-cubes to length using the sled on the tablesaw (see **photo 5-3**). This operation can also be done using a handsaw and cutoff box as shown on page 24, but it is difficult for a novice to get as accurate a cut as is required. A stop block clamped to the sled controls the exact length of the cut. I use the eraser end of a pencil to hold the stock in place during the cut and to move it out of the way for the next cut after the sled is pulled back into its starting position (see **photo 5-4**). Sand and finish the pieces, if desired.

Photo 5-3. Cut the cubes using a sled and stop block to control the length of cut.

Photo 5-4. Use the same setup to cut the triangles of both sizes to the required length.

Historically Speaking:
Evolution of Blocks

Some critics of kindergarten insisted that halved and quartered blocks were too small for manipulation by kindergarten-age children—that their size made them too hard to handle and stack. So many later kindergartens made use of much larger blocks that allowed for play to be more of a social engagement rather than individualized play.

Making the Gift 5 Box

PARTS LIST *for the* GIFT 5 FINGER-JOINTED BOX

Number	Part Name	Dimensions	Material
2	Low sides	$5/16$ x $3 1/16$ x $3 3/4$ in.	Basswood*
2	High sides	$5/16$ x $3 3/8$ x $3 3/4$ in.	Basswood*
1	Bottom	$1/8$ x $3 3/4$ x $3 3/4$ in.	Baltic birch plywood
1	Lid	$5/16$ x $3 9/32$ x $3 3/4$ in.	Basswood*

*or other medium-density hardwood

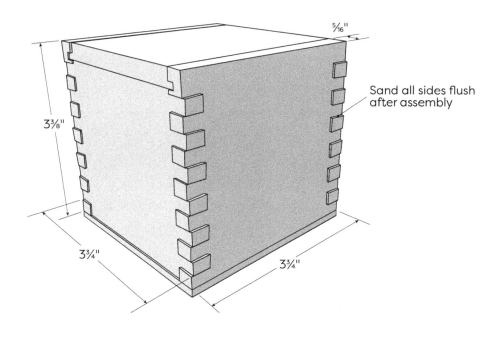

$5/16$"

Sand all sides flush after assembly

$3 3/8$"

$3 3/4$"

$3 3/4$"

PARTS LIST *for the* GIFT 5 NAILED BOX

Number	Part Name	Dimensions	Material
2	Low sides	$3/8$ x $3 1/16$ x $3 1/16$ in.	White pine*
2	High sides	$1/4$ x $3 5/16$ x $3 13/16$ in.	White pine*
1	Bottom	$1/8$ x $3 9/16$ x $3 13/16$ in.	Baltic birch plywood
1	Lid	$1/8$ x $3 5/8$ x $4 1/16$ in.	Baltic birch plywood

*or other softwood

Froebel's kindergarten gift 5 (and the upcoming 5B and 6) are much more complex than the earlier gifts. They each fit in the same size box, and the importance of the box to hold all the parts for storage and reuse becomes increasingly clear with these larger sets. By arranging blocks into layers, they can be stacked, the upside-down box can be placed over them, and the whole set can be slid onto the lid. When turned upright, the lid can be slid into place and the blocks put away.

The box for this gift is made in exactly the same manner as the box for gifts 3 and 4, except that the boxes are 1 inch larger in dimension in each direction and hold over three times as many blocks. If you want to create a finger-jointed box, use the parts list here and follow the directions on page 54, except note that you will need eight ¾-inch

Photo 5-5. Here is a great example of a box for gift 5 submitted by John Kinnear.

#19 nails or a pin-nailer. If you'd prefer a nailed box, use the parts list here and follow the directions on page 28. Do not feel limited by the box designs presented here—choose your own woods and make the project your own (see **photo 5-5**).

GIFT 5B

[Cubes and Cylinders]

Photos by Danielle Atkins

MATERIALS

- Wood,
  see parts list
- Shellac or
  clear Danish oil,
  if desired

TOOLS

- Router with ½-in.
  radius roundover
  bit and ½-in.
  radius cove bit
- Tablesaw with
  sled and blade
- Push stick
- Clamp
- Stop block
- Pencil with eraser
- Sanding block

Followers of Froebel introduced gift 5B, which is similar to gift 5 but also includes half-round shapes and cubes with coves cut into a corner. Making the blocks for gift 5B is a bit more complex, but the set provides the blocks required to build Romanesque arches and simple columns associated with medieval architecture, making this one of my favorite sets. The box for gift 5B is the same as the box for gift 5 (see page 72).

The introduction of half-cylinders in this gift provides the opportunity for building columns and reintroduces the cylinder shape from its much earlier use in gift 2. The square with a cove removed is suggestive of the arch and requires very careful attention to balance as the child builds new forms. Part of Froebel's intention was to connect the child with both the world of nature and the world of man; that transition can be seen in the child's use of gift 5 to build forms even more strongly anchored in the world of architecture.

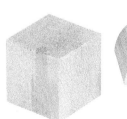

GIFT 5B—THINGS YOU CAN MAKE

FORMS OF LIFE

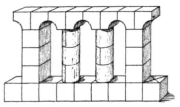

Ruins of a cloister.

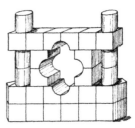

A portion of a wall.

Ancient city gate.

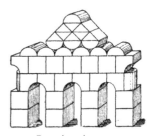

Royal archway.

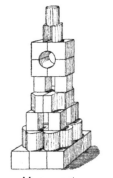

Monument.

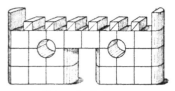

Gate of a fortress.

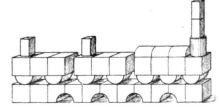

Railroad train on bridge.

Railroad station.

FORMS OF KNOWLEDGE

Welbé, Paradise of Childhood.

FORMS OF BEAUTY

Welbé, Paradise of Childhood.

Making Gift 5B

PARTS LIST *for* GIFT 5B

	Number	Part Name	Dimensions	Material
	12	Whole cubes	1 x 1 x 1 in.	White pine or basswood
	12	Quarter-cubes	1 x 1 x 1 in. cube divided from corner to corner twice	White pine or basswood
	12	Half-cylinders	1-in. long x ½-in. thick	White pine or basswood
	8	Cove pieces	1 x 1 x 1 in. cube with quarter-round removed	White pine or basswood

> **⚠ WARNING**
> The smaller size blocks in this gift can present a choking hazard and should be used only by older children.

Make Half-Round Blocks

I begin by using a ½-inch roundover bit in the router to form a rounded edge on a piece of 1-inch thick stock. Simply rout on one edge and then flip the stock over to rout the opposite side. The bearing on the roundover bit will follow the edge to form a half-round shape (see **photo 5B-1**). Then, use the tablesaw to cut the half-round shape from the 1-inch thick stock (see **photo 5B-2**). I set the fence ½-inch from the blade to make this cut.

Rout the Cove-Cornered Blocks

Routing the cove-cornered blocks requires a change of router bit. Set the depth of a ½-inch cove bit so that it cuts ½-inch deep along the edge of the stock. I prefer to use stock wide enough that it can be safely clamped to the workbench. Then, run the router along the edge (see **photo 5B-3**). Plan for your remaining stock to be cut into cubes to finish the set

After the routing is complete, set the tablesaw fence 1 inch from the blade and cut a strip of stock for cove-cornered blocks (see **photo 5B-4**).

Cut the Blocks to Length

Use the tablesaw and sled to finish the cove-cornered and half-round blocks, as well as cubes and quarter-cubes to finish the set (see page 70). Again, the stop block controls the length of the cut and I use the eraser end of a pencil to hold the block in place throughout the cut (see **photo 5B-5**). Sand the blocks and apply finish, if desired.

Photo 5B-1. To begin forming the half-round blocks for gift 5B, use a router with a ½-inch radius roundover bit and 1-inch thick stock. Rout on one side and then the other using the bearing on the bit to guide the router along the edge.

Photo 5B-4. Cut the cove blocks from the edge of the stock using the tablesaw with the fence set 1 inch from the blade.

Photo 5B-2. Set the fence ½-inch from the blade to cut the half-round from the edge of the board. Have a push stick handy to help guide the half-round piece through the end of the cut.

Photo 5B-3. Use a similar approach to form the cove-cornered blocks. Use a router with a ½-inch radius cove bit and guide bearing to rout the cove along one edge of 1-inch-thick stock.

Photo 5B-5. Use the tablesaw and sled to cut the cove-cornered and half-round blocks to their finished length.

Making Cove-Cornered and Half-Round Blocks by Hand

Making cove-cornered blocks by hand requires a gouge of the correct radius to make the cut. This type of tool was common in Froebel's day, and while I cannot be certain that he and his followers made their blocks for gift 5B in the same manner that I demonstrate here, if you have straight-grained stock to work with, the gouge can turn regular cubes into cove-cornered blocks in a few quick strokes. You will need eight of these blocks to make a set, so plan to make extras and use the best you've cut in your finished set.

TOOLS

- Handsaw
- Miter box
- Compass
- Marking gauge
- Gouge, ½-in. radius
- Mallet
- Chisel or carving knife

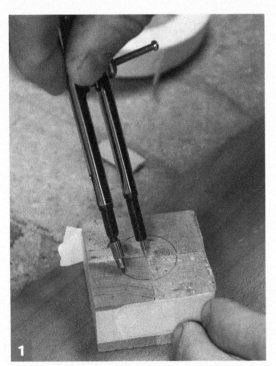

1 Cut blocks using a handsaw and miter box. Then, use a compass to mark the cove. I tape four blocks together, center the pin of the compass into the intersection between blocks, and scribe an arc on all four blocks with a ½-inch radius. I do this on both ends to make sure that the blocks are well marked and that the cove is the same on both sides. Notice that I am marking on end grain.

2 Next, use a marking gauge set at ½-inch to mark the center of the blocks from one end to the other. These marking gauge lines are important for making sure the cove cut is equidistant from the edges of the blocks.

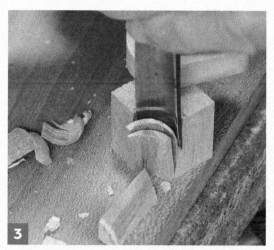

3 Use a ½-inch radius gouge and mallet to begin forming the cove cut. Cutting in small increments will give greater accuracy.

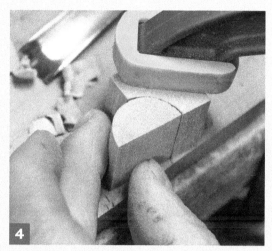

4 To make the half-round column blocks with handtools, simply cut cubes to length and then mark the ½-inch radius on each end and whittle them to shape. You can use either a chisel or knife. Use one to test the fit of the other.

Photo by Danielle Atkins

[Whole and Divided Tiles]

MATERIALS

- Wood,
  see parts list
- Masking tape,
  optional

TOOLS

- Tablesaw
  with blade
- Sled
- Stop block
- Pencil with eraser

Gift 6 is a more complex version of gift 4, but is almost as easy to make. Like the transition from gift 3 to gift 4, the transition from 5 to 6 is from cubes and variations to flat tiles more similar to bricks. Instead of eight tiles, there are 36 total pieces, including tiles that have been cut in half to make two squares, and tiles that have been cut in half to make thin columns. Balancing the thin columns on end can require just a bit more dexterity, and gift 6 adds new design opportunities that keep the child from getting bored. Six layers of tiles form a 3-inch cube. The box is slightly larger to accommodate the increase in pieces; the box for gift 6

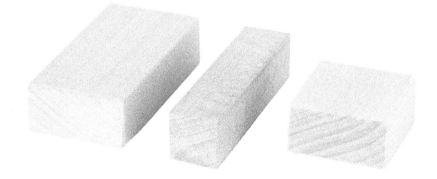

Photos by Danielle Atkins

PARTS LIST FOR GIFT 6

	Number	Part Name	Dimensions	Material
	18	Whole tiles	½ x 1 x 2 in.	Basswood*
	12	Square half tiles	½ x 1 x 1 in.	Basswood*
	6	Column half tiles	½ x ½ x 2 in.	Basswood*

*or other medium-density hardwood

is the same as the box for gift 5 (see page 72). For crafting this gift, power tools are preferred. Follow the directions on page 53, adjusting the stop block as needed to modify the size of the tiles. Sand the tiles when complete (see **photo 6-1**) and finish if desired.

Photo 6-1. Use sticky-back sandpaper glued to a board to provide an effective sanding surface for your blocks.

GIFT 6 — THINGS YOU CAN MAKE

FORM OF LIFE

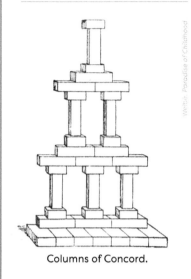

Columns of Concord.

FORMS OF KNOWLEDGE

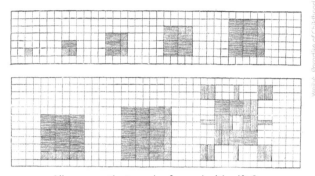

All squares that can be formed with gift 6.

FORMS OF BEAUTY

GIFT 7

[Drawing Tiles]

MATERIALS

- Wood,
  see parts list
- Masking or
  painter's tape
- Shellac or
  clear Danish oil,
  if desired

TOOLS

- Tablesaw with
  blade, fence, miter
  gauge, and sled
- Stop block
- Clamp
- Pencil with eraser
- Sanding block

Because Froebel's gift 7 represents not solids, but surfaces, it was intended to help pupils develop skills in design, and to build upon the complexity of the tools offered in the previous gifts. Students use the tiles to draw, but unlike the drawing that most children do today with colored pencils and crayons, the use of objects to do that drawing make it more ordered and architectural in its application. The tiles could be arranged and rearranged on a tabletop to make whatever a child might imagine, or with guidance, could be used to make the same kinds of beauty forms made by the students with gifts 3, 4, 5, 5B, and 6.

The number of parts in gift 7 was nearly double the number of parts in the earlier gifts. I created 48 of each type of tile, with a separate box for each tile type. That is only a suggestion—make as many or few types of tiles as you like. Also, gift 7 was offered by manufacturers in several options; the book *Paradise of Childhood* actually recommended five tile types, each type kept separately in its own box: square tiles (see **photo 7-1**), right-angle triangles with two equal sides (half of a square) (see **photo 7-2**), right-angle triangles with unequal sides (see **photo 7-3**), equilateral triangles (see **photo 7-4**), and obtuse-angled triangles with two equal sides (see **photo 7-5**). Squares are useful for continuing to build

Photo 7-1. Square tiles can be used in the same manner as the cubes from earlier gifts to create forms of beauty, but the number of tiles makes amazingly complex arrangements possible.

Photo 7-2. Right triangles with two equal sides are similar in design potential to the triangular blocks from gifts 5, 5B, and 6.

Photo 7-3. Right angle triangles with unequal sides can be used to create both curved and rectilinear forms.

Photo 7-4. Equilateral triangles offer an interesting alternative to the forms made from square tiles.

Photo 7-5. Obtuse triangles with two equal sides offer additional abstract forms and geometric arrangements.

upon gift 3, whereas the triangles introduce the creation of curves and spirals. Having that many different versions of the gift 7 was probably more complicated than Froebel intended, and you may not wish to make all the shapes.

But as complicated as all this may seem, regulating the way the tiles are introduced brings some simplicity. For instance, the book *Paradise of Childhood* recommended that the teacher introduce the gift by giving the child only three like tiles to start, so that he or she might exhaust the full range of possible designs before more tiles were added to the set and more complex patterns became possible. When all the design options were discovered using just three tiles, the set would be expanded to six, then nine, and so on. As you can imagine, the growing complexity and variety of forms available would grow exponentially, and through the exercise of these various forms, it was expected that the child's creativity in the use of the tiles might also grow.

Historically Speaking:
Froebel's Crystallography Background

Another experience that had a profound impact on Froebel's development of his gifts was when he was appointed to serve as an assistant to Professor Christian Samuel Weiss in the mineralogical museum in Berlin. Professor Weiss was one of the foremost crystallographers of his time. Froebel wrote of his experience, "My duties busied me the greater part of the day amongst minerals, dumb witnesses to the silent thousand-fold creative energy of nature....Geology and crystallography not only opened up for me a higher circle of knowledge and insight, but also showed me a higher goal for my inquiry, my speculation, and my endeavor." He speculated that the same order and symmetry that could be found in crystals was also present in the rest of life. The tablets of gift 7, in various triangular shapes and in a square form, could be arranged in forms reminiscent of those Froebel had witnessed both in nature and through his time working in the mineralogical laboratory. It would make sense from a mineralogical design standpoint to see how various shapes of triangle might lead to various types of form, as each type does lend itself to distinctive designs.

Historically Speaking:

Gift 7

According to editor's notes from the quarter-century edition of the *Paradise of Childhood,* "As the tablets of the seventh gift represent surfaces instead of solids, they at once become more ideal and serve as an introduction to the elements of drawing, or to the representation of solids by plane surfaces. These tablets, in fact, contain in concrete form the principles of plain geometry, and illustrate many of the problems in elementary industrial drawing. The natural foundation for a mathematical and scientific education which the kindergarten lays is an important element to aid in the production of more expert and accurate workmen in any manual occupation, and will tend to cultivate a more accurate and practical conception of everyday experiences."

Utilizing Gift 7

In the earliest days of kindergarten, classes had been small. By the time kindergartens were entering the arena of public education in the 1880s and were being adapted to compete head to head with more standard means of education, class sizes were pushed upward to as many as 50 students. The challenge for teachers to manage gifts with so many parts in each must have been difficult. And so, perhaps the best use of these gifts is not with huge classes, but within families and in small school settings where each student can be given individual attention.

Various teachers would find better use for some triangular tiles of gift 7 than others, so with regard to the purchase of sets for classrooms, editor's notes in the *Paradise of Childhood* pointed out that there was some discussion as to which set or sets would provide the greatest benefit to the growing child. Teachers often chose which would work best for them rather than invest in multiple sets, or might have several different sets that students could use following the Froebel model of self-activity.

GIFT 7—THINGS YOU CAN MAKE

FORMS OF LIFE

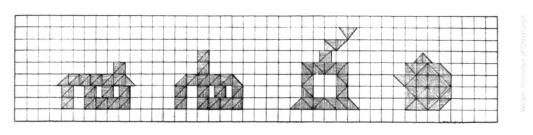

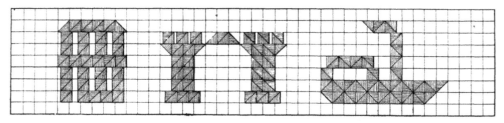

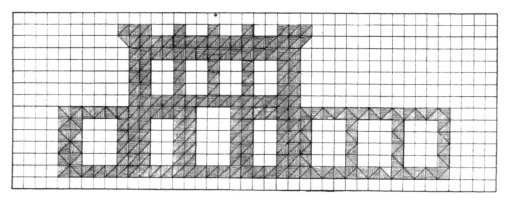

FORMS OF KNOWLEDGE

FORMS OF BEAUTY

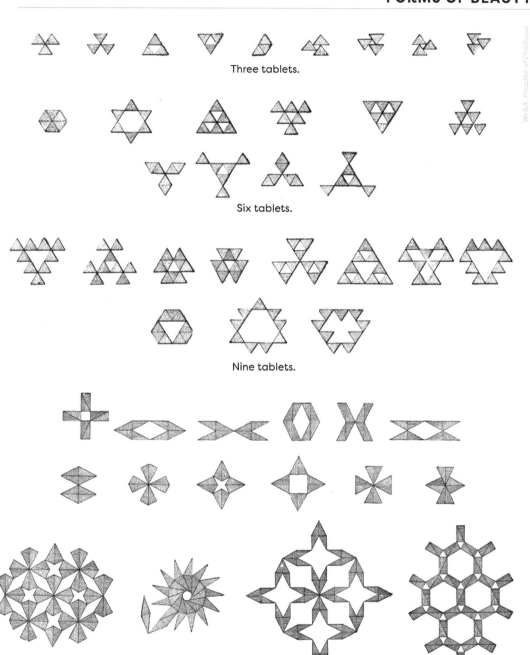

Three tablets.

Six tablets.

Nine tablets.

Making Gift 7

PARTS LIST *for* GIFT 7

	Number	Part Name	Dimensions	Material
▢	36–48	Square tiles	⅛ x 1 x 1 in.	White pine or basswood*
◺	36–48	Right-angle triangle tiles with two equal sides (one 90° and two 45° angles)	⅛ x ¾ x 1½ in.	White pine or basswood
◿	36–48	Right-angle triangle tiles with unequal sides (one 30°, one 60°, and one 90° angle)	⅛ x ¾ x 1¼ in.	White pine or basswood
△	36–48	Equilateral triangle tiles (each angle is 60°)	⅛ x 1 x 1 in.	White pine or basswood
◁	36–48	Obtuse-angle triangle tiles with two equal sides (one 110° and two 35° angles)	⅛ x ¾ x 2 in.	White pine or basswood

*Make whichever sets you prefer; you do not need to make all of these shapes.

Tape the Stock Together

The dimension of the strips is ⅛ x 1 inch; the length of the strips is not critical, except that for ripping on the saw, they should be about 18 inches or longer for safety of handling. Making the tiles used in gift 7 is best accomplished using modern tablesaw techniques, and I make it easier for myself by using tape to hold thin stock together in layers so that several pieces can be cut at the same time (see **photo 7-6**). Even if you intend to carefully cut triangular and square tiles via handtool techniques, the taped bundle of layers will speed up your work.

Cut the Tiles

I use the sled on the tablesaw to cut the square tablets to length, and use the miter gauge on the tablesaw to cut the triangles to size and shape. Align the bundle of thin strips to touch the block clamped to the tablesaw fence (see **photo 7-7**). Note that in **photo 7-8** the miter gauge and stock have moved away from the block, creating an open space between the tablets and the fence. This is to prevent the dangerous situation called *trapping* in which stock is between the blade and fence and gets chewed up and thrown at the operator. The eraser end of a pencil can be used to keep the stock under complete control during the cut and to move it carefully aside for the next cut (see **photo 7-9**).

The equilateral triangles, right-angle triangles with equal sides, and obtuse-angle triangles with two equal sides can be made in the same manner (see **photo 7-10**). The right-angle triangles with unequal sides require both an angle cut using the miter gauge and a second 90° cut using the sled. See the parts list for the necessary angles. Sand the edges of the pieces so there are no splinters, and apply a finish if desired.

Photo 7-6. Rip the material for tablets into thin strips and then tape them together so that several can be cut safely at the same time. This technique is helpful whether you are cutting tiles with handtools or with the tablesaw.

Photo 7-7. Use the miter gauge on the tablesaw to cut the tablets to shape. Use a block clamped to the tablesaw fence well back from the blade as your stop block.

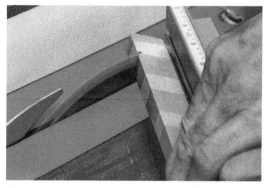

Photo 7-8. As the miter gauge moves the stock forward into the cut, an opening is left so that the stock is not trapped between the fence and blade.

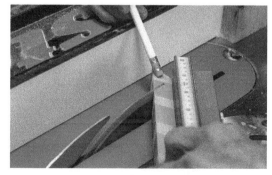

Photo 7-9. Use a pencil with eraser to control the tiles as they are cut from the stock. With my hand sliding securely along the fence and a safe distance from the blade, the pencil keeps the triangles from being thrown back by the blade.

Photo 7-10. Change the angle of the miter gauge to cut the various triangle shapes you select.

Making the Gift 7 Box

PARTS LIST *for the* **GIFT 7 FINGER-JOINTED BOX**

Number	Part Name	Dimensions	Material
2	Low sides	⁵⁄₁₆ x 1⅛ x 3⅛ in.	Basswood
2	High sides	⁵⁄₁₆ x 1⁷⁄₁₆ x 5⅛ in.	Basswood
1	Bottom	⅛ x 3⅛ x 5⅛ in.	Baltic birch plywood
1	Lid	⁵⁄₁₆ x 2²³⁄₃₂ x 5⅛ in.	Basswood

MATERIALS

- Wood,
  see parts list
- ½-in. #19 nails, 8*

*Pin-nailer may be used in place of real nails

PARTS LIST *for the* **GIFT 7 NAILED BOX**

Number	Part Name	Dimensions	Material
2	Low sides	⅜ x 1⅛ x 2½ in.	White pine*
2	High sides	¼ x 1⅜ x 5⅛ in.	White pine*
1	Bottom	⅛ x 3 x 5⅛ in.	Baltic birch plywood
1	Lid	⅛ x 2²³⁄₃₂ x 5½ in.	Baltic birch plywood

*or other softwood

MATERIALS

- Wood,
  see parts list
- ⅝-in. #19 nails, 18*

*Pin-nailer may be used in place of real nails

The box for gift 7 need not fit an exact cube as in the earlier gifts, for it would be far too difficult to gather the parts into a cube shape for storage. A low rectangular box and sliding lid made using either the finger-jointed or nailed techniques from the box for gift 3 will be helpful.

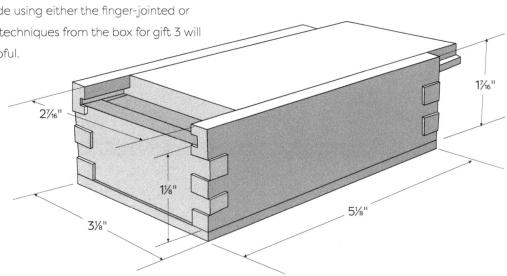

Making a Play Board

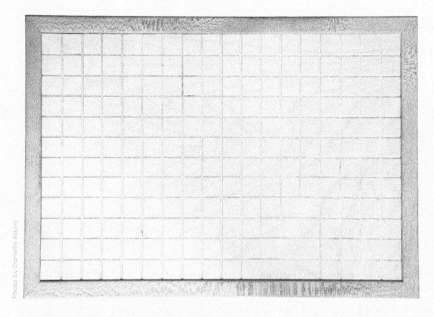

Photo by Danielle Atkins

MATERIALS
- Wood,
  see parts list
- Glue

TOOLS
- Router table
  with V-groove bit
- Disc sander or
  sanding block
- Tablesaw with
  blade, fence,
  and miter gauge
- Stop block
- Clamps

In many early kindergartens, special tables were made with a grid pattern routed or drawn on the top. This grid guided the student in the careful arrangement of blocks. Another option is to make a play board that can be used on any table. For mine, I made a surface from ¼-inch Baltic birch plywood and a border from light-colored hardwood. Use a V-groove router bit in the router table with the tip raised only 1⁄16-inch above the surface.

PARTS LIST *for* PLAY BOARD

Number	Part Name	Dimensions	Material
1	Play board surface	¼ x 13½ x 19½ in.	Baltic birch plywood
2	Long border pieces	¾ x 1 x 20 in.	Light-colored hardwood
2	Short border pieces	¾ x 1 x 14 in.	Light-colored hardwood

Making a Play Board, *continued*

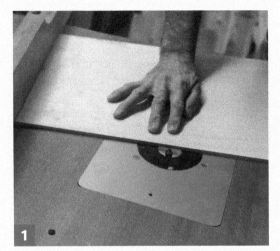

1 Start routing straight lines at the center of the board, and then move the fence in 1-inch increments to form the grid.

2 The routing should be planned to allow for a wider border along the edge.

3 Pass the edge of the stock between the tablesaw blade and fence to form a tongue ⅛-inch-thick on the edge of the stock to fit a groove cut in the border. Then sand the surface flat on both sides.

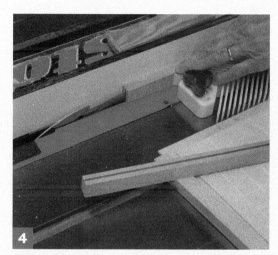

Cut into the edge of the hardwood border stock. The depth of the cut should equal the width of the tongue on the edge of the plywood stock. Sand the surface of the board.

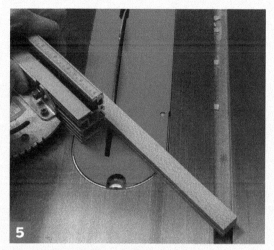

Use a miter gauge on the tablesaw to cut the border stock to fit around the plywood. A stop block on the miter gauge is used to make certain matching parts are cut exactly the same length.

Apply glue to the miters and just a bit in the grooves at each end, then clamp the edges to the play board.

GIFT 8

[Drawing Sticks]

MATERIALS

- Wood,
  see parts list

TOOLS

- Tablesaw
  with blade,
  fence, and sled

- Compound
  miter saw or miter
  box, optional

- Push stick

- Fine-grit
  sandpaper

- Nontoxic markers,
  if desired

- Stop block

Gift 8 consists of straight sticks for drawing the outlines of shapes; even before children are able to hold a pencil or pen, they are able to place pieces of gift 8 on a table or board to create shapes. While the earlier gifts have involved the use of blocks and tablets to create form, the use of sticks to draw moves the child's development in a more abstract direction. To draw is more representational than to build with blocks, and so the child moves in small steps from the concrete to the abstract.

For many children not of sufficient age to hold a pen or pencil in the required manner, drawing with sticks is easier, and because the sticks can be readily rearranged, the child is not hindered in his or her creativity by marking up real paper. Forms of knowledge include basic addition and subtraction with the sticks.

I chose to make the sticks from wood, but you could use wire if you wanted to match gift 9. As this gift and the rest from here to the end of the book were made by various craftsmen in communities in every country in which kindergarten was introduced, there are no exact size requirements. I have included my recommendations, but choose the sizes you think are best and that work best for your child. The box for gift 7 is a good size for gift 8 (see page 96).

Photo by Danielle Atkins

Historically Speaking:
Drawing with Concrete Items

Froebel believed that children should begin drawing with concrete things. Just as some art teachers will instruct their students to look for geometric forms within the forms of nature, the study of form would build the child's capacity to design, even before he or she was able to manage pen and pencil on paper. The rule, as stated by Otto Salomon to his students, was that learning should move from the concrete to the abstract.

Making Gift 8

PARTS LIST *for* GIFT 8

	Number	Part Name	Dimensions	Material
	20–25	Sticks	⅛ x ⅛ x 5 in.	Basswood or pine

Rip the Sticks

To make the sticks, I use the tablesaw to rip thin ⅛-inch strips from ⁵⁄₁₆-inch basswood or pine (see **photo 8-1**). A push stick is required to safely guide the stock through the cut. After cutting as many strips as you like, leave the tablesaw fence in place and lower the saw blade; turn the strips flat and cut them into skinnier sticks (see **photo 8-2**).

Finish the Sticks

Use fine-grit sandpaper to sand the edges of each strip smooth to the touch. At this point, use nontoxic markers to color the square stock or leave the sticks natural (see **photo 8-3**). If you do color the sticks, be sure to let them dry. Gather the sticks into bundles; masking tape holds them together for a safer, more accurate cut. Use a tablesaw with sled, a compound miter saw, or a miter box and saw to cut the sticks to length; I chose to make my sticks 5 inches long (see **photo 8-4**). Use a stop block to control the length of the sticks.

Photo 8-1. Use the tablesaw to rip thin strips.

Photo 8-2. Lower the height of the blade and cut the strips into square stock.

Photo 8-3. You may choose to color your sticks with nontoxic markers or leave them natural.

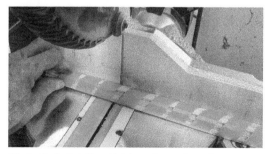

Photo 8-4. Cut the stick bundles to length.

GIFT 8—THINGS YOU CAN MAKE

FORMS OF LIFE

A dwelling house.

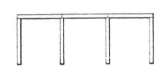

A bridge with three spans.

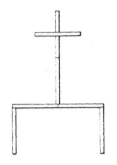

Tombstone and cross.

Webb, Paradise of Childhood.

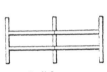

Rail fence.

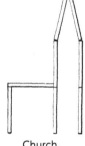

Church.

Gas lantern.

Corn crib.

A flower pot.

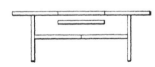

A piano forte.

FORMS OF BEAUTY

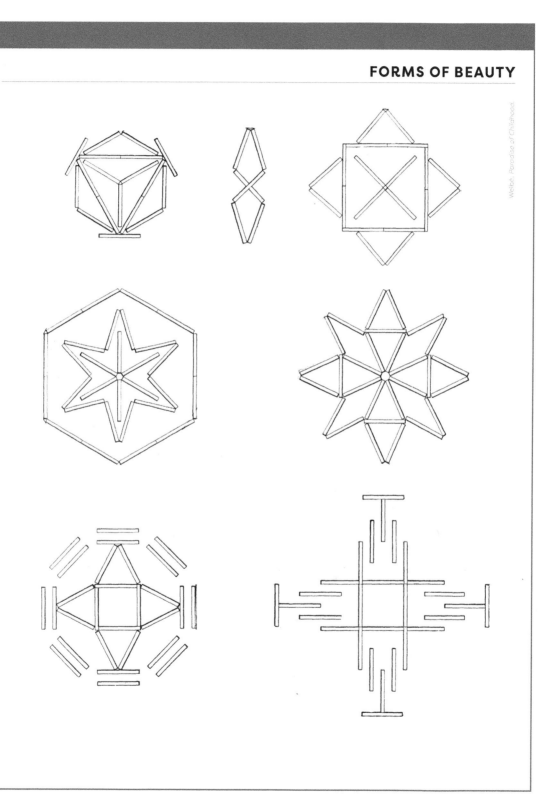

Weibé, *Paradise of Childhood.*

GIFT 9

[Drawing Rings]

MATERIALS
- Bailing wire, see parts list
- Silver solder, if desired

TOOLS
- 1-in. wooden dowel rod
- Wire cutters
- Permanent marker
- Propane torch and vise-grip pliers, if desired
- Drill and ⅛-in. drill bit

Gift 9 has a similar purpose as gift 8, except rings and half-rings are used to draw shapes. The steel rings add another direction in the child's drawing capacity. The use of concrete objects to create abstract representations of forms familiar to the child from his or her observations of nature awaken the child not only to the beauty that surrounds us, but to the child's capacity to create beauty in abstract form. The pieces for this gift are made from steel wire. The box for gift 7 is a good size for gift 9 (see page 96).

PARTS LIST *for* **GIFT 9**

	Number	Part Name	Dimensions	Material
◯	12	Rings	¾-in. diameter	Bailing wire
)	12	Half-rings	Cut from ¾-in. diameter rings	Bailing wire
◯	12	Rings	1¼-in. diameter	Bailing wire
)	12	Half-rings	Cut from 1¼-in. diameter rings	Bailing wire

GIFT 9—THINGS YOU CAN MAKE

FORMS OF LIFE

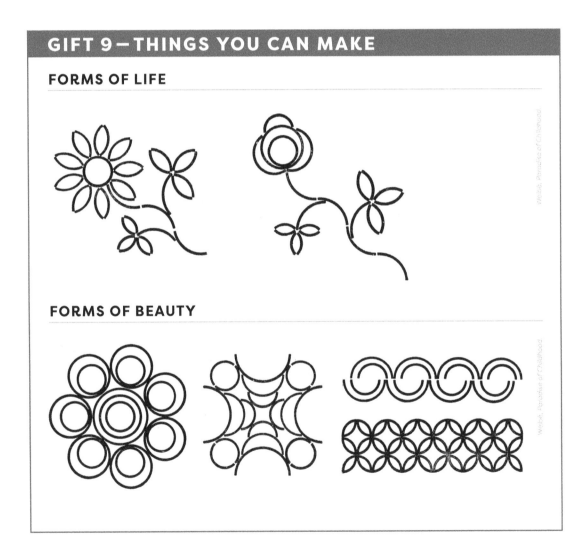

FORMS OF BEAUTY

Make a Wire Coil

To make the rings, purchase common bailing wire from the local hardware store and wrap it tightly around a large wooden dowel. I used ¾- and 1¼-inch diameter dowels. First, drill a hole in a large dowel that is big enough to receive the bailing wire. Insert the loose end of the wire into the hole. Wrap the dowel tightly in wire (see **photo 9-1**). Cut the wire when you have wrapped enough.

Cut the Rings

Mark a line down the length so you will know where to cut to form rings (see **photo 9-2**).

A permanent marker works well for this task. Remove the dowel from the center of the coil of wire and use a wire cutter to separate it into rings (see **photo 9-3**). The rings may be simply aligned at the ends, or you can heat them and apply silver solder to join them on a permanent basis (see **photo 9-4**).

Make the Half-Rings

The half-rings to complete the set are also cut from the coiled wire by marking and cutting more lines on the coil. Use sandpaper to smooth the cut edges.

Photo 9-1. Wind the wire tightly around the dowel.

Photo 9-2. Mark a straight line along one side of the tightly wound wire.

Photo 9-3. Pull the wire coil off the dowel and use wire cutters to cut it into individual rings.

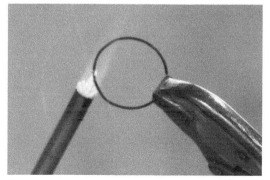

Photo 9-4. Use a propane torch and silver solder to connect the ends of the ring together. This is optional, as the rings will serve the purpose of the gift without being connected.

Photos by Danielle Atkins

GIFT 15

[Weaving Slats]

MATERIALS

- Wood,
  see parts list
- Masking tape,
  optional

TOOLS

- Tablesaw
  with blade
- Sled
- Plane

Gift 15, interlacing or weaving with sticks, is an introduction to weaving in general, and is not as easy to do as one might think. The strips do not interlace as easily as paper or string, and are used to form various geometric shapes. The shapes can be secured with glue at the corners where strips overlap if the child wants to create permanent decorative forms. Gift 15 is made in exactly the same manner as gift 8 (see page 103) but must be cut thinner in order to be flexible enough to be woven. Longer strips offer an advantage, so I cut these to 10 inches long as

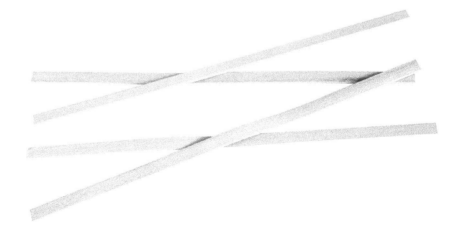

PARTS LIST *for* GIFT 15

	Number	Part Name	Dimensions	Material
	12-24	Slats	$\frac{3}{64}$ x $\frac{5}{16}$ x 10 in.	Basswood or pine

recommended by Edward Weibé's book, the *Paradise of Childhood*. Use the tablesaw to rip thin strips of wood into uniform widths and thicknesses. First, plane the wood to a thickness equal to the desired width ($\frac{5}{16}$-inch) and then use a push stick to safely guide the stock through the tablesaw. Wrap the thin strips with masking tape to make a bundle so that a number of strips can be cut to length at the same time. This will give a cleaner cut in less time, and provide for safe handling of parts. There is no box for this gift.

GIFT 15 — THINGS YOU CAN MAKE

FORMS OF LIFE

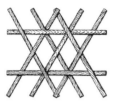  

A fence.   A fence.   A fan.

FORMS OF BEAUTY

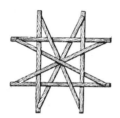 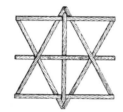 

FORMS OF KNOWLEDGE

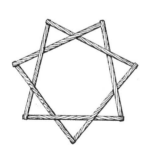 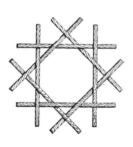 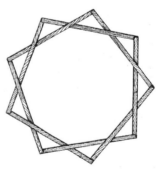

Regular polygons; contemplation of divisions produced by diagonals.

[Joined Sticks]

MATERIALS

- Wood,
  see parts list
- #4 light trimmer
  copper tacks,
  1 per strip

TOOLS

- Router table with
  ⅛-in. roundover bit
- Drill press or
  drill with ¹⁄₁₆-in.
  bit, fence, and
  stop block
- Tack hammer

Gift 16 consists of sticks joined to each other at the ends. The connectors I use are copper tacks clinched on the back side. This gift offers some additional fun, as anyone with an old carpenter's folding rule will know, but it also offers some additional restrictions to the design process. As anyone familiar with the process of design will attest, design happens within sets of limitations that must be mastered and turned to the specific advantage of the finished work. Consider how Frank Lloyd Wright made use of natural settings for his designs; Fallingwater is a classic example. Edward Weibé said of gift 16, "in making simple geometrical figures, the gift is invaluable and the forms of life and beauty which may be produced with it offer profitable exercise for the inventive powers of the child." There is no box for this gift.

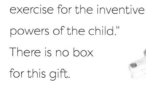

GIFT 16 — THINGS YOU CAN MAKE

FORMS OF LIFE

A house.   A chair.

FORMS OF BEAUTY

Several classes of outlines.

FORMS OF KNOWLEDGE

Making Gift 16

PARTS LIST *for* GIFT 16

	Number	Part Name	Dimensions	Material
⬭	12	Strips	⅛ x ⁵⁄₁₆ x 6 in.	Basswood or pine

After cutting the stock as you did for gifts 8 and 15, bundle them in a stack with masking tape. To make attaching ends, I first use a ⅛-inch-radius roundover bit in the router table to shape the ends. Then, drill through the corners using a ¹⁄₁₆-inch drill bit, which is necessary because the tacks used to attach the ends of the strips would likely split the wood (see **photo 16-1**). I use a fence and stop block to control the position of the holes. Next, drive copper tacks through the holes in two strips to connect the parts (see **photos 16-2** and **16-3**). I use #4 light trimmer tacks that are commonly used in making oval Shaker boxes. They are almost ½-inch long, which allows them to be clinched on the opposite side. The gift is now ready to be arranged into a variety of shapes (see **photo 16-4**).

Photo 16-1. Use a drill press to drill through the bundled stock for gift 16.

Photo 16-2. Use copper tacks to secure the ends of the sticks to each other. Fit the tack in the hole and use a tack hammer to bend down the end.

Photo 16-3. The copper tacks are seen here from the front side.

Photo 16-4. The tacks allow the sticks in gift 16 to be arranged in a variety of shapes.

Froebel's Occupations

The difference between what Froebel himself called a *gift* and what he termed an *occupation* was that the gift was used and learned from and then put away unchanged. The occupation was the child's opportunity to change the materials to reflect his or her own self-activity and creative inclinations. Students can use pencils and paper to draw, model things from clay, use scissors to cut out paper shapes, weave strips of paper or string, use needles, thread, and paper to make designs and learn to sew, and construct geometric shapes with thin sticks and dried peas in much the same way TinkerToys are used (see **photo O-1**).

Purpose of the Occupations

While the gifts provided an opportunity for the child to learn about the universe, the

Photo O-1. Learning to sew with needle, thread, and paper, as well as weaving with wooden and paper strips, are both occupations.

occupations gave the child the opportunity to construct more permanent expressions of mind, and engage in a creative dialog with reality. The idea of occupations fits well with Froebel's theory of self-activity: the child is not only to take in knowledge as presented by others, but to test learning in his or her own hands, and express learning through personal creativity.

The occupations were not intended to lead a child toward a career like carpentry or the arts, but were intended by Froebel to build the child's mind, attention, and dexterity in ways that would be useful in any real occupation of the time. Instead, he introduced children to the various real occupations they would find practiced by adults in their communities through his book, *Mother Play (Mutter und Kose Lieder)*, which has pictures illustrating the work and importance of various members of the community. These included the carpenter, the baker, and even the lowly charcoal maker (see **figure O-1**), pointing out his important role in warming the home and providing fuel for the blacksmith.

As a parent or teacher, your job is simply to provide the materials and necessary tools for the child to create and then find time to serve as a role model with your own creativity. Trust your child to follow from that point. It also makes great sense to establish a place in your home where you and your child or children can work with basic tools like scissors, and materials in the form of paper and string.

These days, parents are lured into buying things for their children that provide little opportunity for the actual exercise of their child's creativity. Even the toys that make claims of being educational and creativity-inspiring may pale in comparison to what your child may discover with his or her own hands.

Gift 10

Gift 10 as illustrated in the *Paradise of Childhood* consists of the child creating patterns by drawing horizontal and vertical lines on graph paper with colored pencils, as seen in **figure O-2**. This seems very simple, but

Figure O-1. An illustration from Froebel's book, *Mother Play*, shows the charcoal maker's occupation.

Historically Speaking:

Occupations

A bit of confusion could result from Edward Weibé's book *Paradise of Childhood* as he referred in it to occupations as gifts and failed to clearly distinguish between the two forms.

Froebel recognized it as being a transition from drawing with objects to drawing with pen or pencil.

Edward Weibé wrote of this occupation in *Paradise of Childhood*, "It was Froebel's task to invent a method adapted to the tender age of the child, and his slight dexterity of hand, and in the meantime to satisfy the claim of all his occupations, *ie.*, that the child should not simply imitate, but proceed self-actingly, to perform work which enables him to reflect, reason, and finally to invent himself." The gift of drawing, as any artist would know, can be refined from a simple starting point of using guidelines on paper to unrestricted creativity without limit as the child learns skills of observation and dexterity of both mind and hand.

Gifts 11 and 12

The gifts or occupations 11 and 12 use needle and thread-lined paper to begin the crafts of perforating and embroidering (see **figure O-3**). In perforating (gift 11), the student would simply make patterns of holes on lined paper. These would later be connected through the use of embroidery floss in gift 12.

Gift 13

Gift 13 in *Paradise of Childhood* is identified as "Material for cutting paper and mounting pieces to produce figures and form." By cutting and gluing papers of interesting colors, beautiful patterns can be formed. Again, either forms of beauty or representational shapes could be formed (see **figure O-4**).

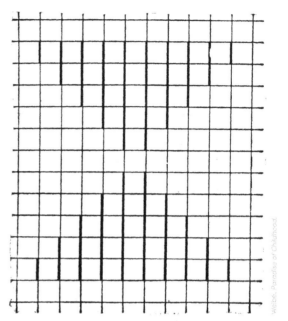

Figure O-2. Gift 10 as shown in *Paradise of Childhood* was simply drawing straight lines to make patterns.

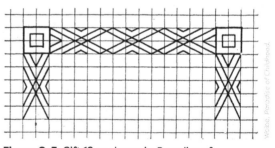

Figure O-3. Gift 12 as shown in *Paradise of Childhood* was basic embroidery.

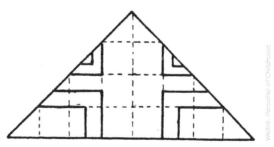

Figure O-4. Gift 13 as shown in *Paradise of Childhood* was cutting and gluing paper shapes.

Gift 14

Edward Weibé in *Paradise of Childhood* identified "material for braiding and weaving" as Froebel's 14th gift (see **figure O-5**). Paper weaving remains popular as a kindergarten activity throughout the world. Use scissors to cut strips of colorful paper; fold a piece of construction paper in half; cut from the center outward, being careful not to cut all the way (see **photo O-2**). Weaving the brightly colored strips through this loom paper is an easy way to experiment with color and make art. I found gift 14 prominently displayed among kindergarten artifacts from the early 20th century in the Trøndelag Sverresborg Folk Museum in Trondheim, Norway (see **photo O-3**).

Gifts 15 and 16

Gifts 15 and 16 are made of materials that can be made by a woodworker and can go back to their original form without permanent alteration, so I have covered the making of those gifts separately in the text.

Weibé, *Paradise of Childhood*.

Figure O-5. Gift 14 as shown in *Paradise of Childhood*.

Photo O-2. Gift 14 is paper weaving. To prepare material for your child, simply make cuts in paper as shown and cut strips of various colors to use in creating a woven design.

Photo O-3. Weaving projects displayed at the Trøndelag Sverresborg Folk Museum. Individual teachers around the world working with small groups of kindergarten students found interesting ways to build upon Froebel's gifts, such as these woven miniature pieces of furniture.

Gifts 17 and 18

Gift 17, which Edward Weibé called "material for intertwining," consists of paper strips that could be cut for the child's use, but that could also be cut by the child for his or her own use. Interesting forms could be devised by the child by strategically folding paper into various designs (see **figure O-6**). Gift 18 could be viewed as a simple precursor for origami. Gift 18 involved cutting and folding paper into new forms, and would later become a part of a school craft called *paper sloyd* that was used to prepare students for wood shop (see **figure O-7**).

Gift 19

In the occupation sticks and peas (or peas-work), children would soften dried peas in water and connect them with toothpicks

(continued on page 126)

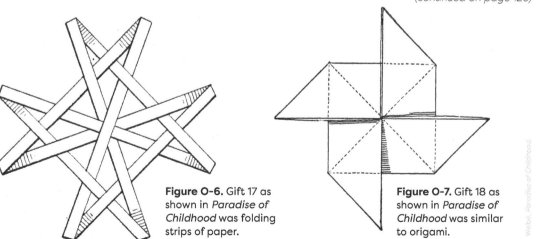

Weibé, *Paradise of Childhood.*

Figure O-6. Gift 17 as shown in *Paradise of Childhood* was folding strips of paper.

Figure O-7. Gift 18 as shown in *Paradise of Childhood* was similar to origami.

Weibé, *Paradise of Childhood.*

Gift 19: Peas and Sticks

MATERIALS

- Wood for box, see parts list
- ⅞-in. #18 nails, 10
- ½-in. #19 nails, 6 (for bottom)
- Cork balls
- Toothpicks

PARTS LIST *for* GIFT 19 BOX

Number	Part Name	Dimensions	Material
2	High sides	¼ x 1¼ x 4 in.	Basswood or white pine
2	Low sides	⅜ x 1 x 3 in.	Basswood or white pine
1	Divider	¼ x ¹⁵⁄₁₆ x 3 in.	Basswood or white pine
1	Bottom	⅛ x 3½ x 4 in.	Baltic birch plywood
1	Lid	⅛ x 3¼ x 4¼ in.	Baltic birch plywood

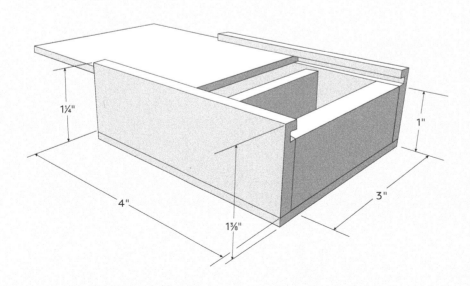

into various forms (see **photo O-4** and **figure O-8**). If using cork balls in place of real dried peas, the parts can be taken apart and put away as was done with the construction gifts. Also, you may want to shorten some toothpicks by cutting them and sharpening the cut ends to increase the creative opportunity. To create a box for gift 19, follow the instructions for the gift 1 box on page 28, but add a divider before attaching the bottom of the box (see **photo O-5**). This will keep the balls separate from the sticks. Also note that I made the lid on this box slightly longer for an easier opening.

Photo O-5. When making a box for sticks and peas, add a divider to create separate compartments.

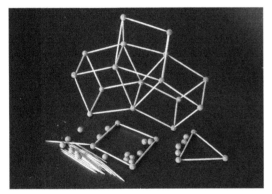

Photo O-4. Small balls of cork can take the place of peas in building triangles and quadrangles to assemble into interesting forms.

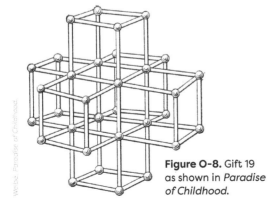

Figure O-8. Gift 19 as shown in *Paradise of Childhood.*

Welbe: Paradise of Childhood.

Historically Speaking:
Buckminster Fuller

Though not intended to guide children to any particular career, for some students the occupations had a profound effect on what they would do later in life. Buckminster Fuller was nearly blind as a child, and wore thick glasses as an adult. In kindergarten, while the other children used sticks and peas to construct rectilinear shapes, Fuller, being unfamiliar with rectilinear shapes and unable to clearly see what he was doing, found particular strength in forming triangles. This led later to his invention of the geodesic dome.

Gift 20

Gift 20 simply consists of modeling clay or wax, a wooden knife, a board, and an oiled paper (or we may use wax paper now) to serve as a work surface. In addition to learning to shape the clay, children develop a sense of cleanliness and care in order to prevent soiling their hands and clothing. The clay forms that the child creates should be dried in the sun or a warm oven to harden (see **figure O-9**).

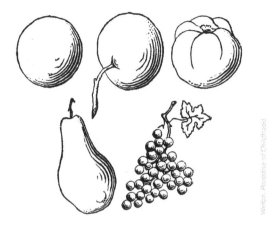

Figure O-9. Gift 20, modeling clay, as shown in *Paradise of Childhood.*

Historically Speaking:
The Imagination of Children

Mademoiselle Albertine Necker de Saussure wrote the following in the early 1800s: "It is a matter of surprise to some, that children are satisfied with the rudest imitations. They are looked down upon for their want of feeling for art, while they should rather be admired for the force of imagination that renders such illusion possible. Mold a lump of wax into a figure or cut one out of paper, and, provided it has something like legs and arms and a rounded piece for a head, it will be a man in the eyes of the child. This man will last for weeks; the loss of a limb or two will make no difference; and he will fill every part you choose to make him play. The child does not see the imperfect copy, but only the model in his own mind. The wax figure is to him only a symbol on which he does not dwell. No matter though the symbol be ill chosen and insignificant; the young spirit penetrates the veil, arrives at the thing itself, and contemplates it in its true aspect. Too exact imitations of things undergo the fate of the things themselves, of which the child soon tires. He admires them, is delighted with them, but his imagination is impeded by the exactness of their forms, which represent one thing only; and how is he to be contented with one amusement? A toy soldier fully equipped is only a soldier; it can not represent his father or any other personage. It would seem as if the young mind felt its originality more strongly when, under the inspiration of the moment, it puts all things in requisition, and sees, in everything around, the instruments of its pleasure. A stool turned over is a boat, a carriage; set on its legs it becomes a horse or a table; a bandbox becomes a house, a cupboard, a wagon—anything. You should enter into his ideas, and, even before the time for useful toys, should provide the child with the means of constructing for himself, rather than with things ready made."

Conclusion: The Impact and Legacy of Kindergarten

There has long been a misunderstanding about what Froebel's conceptions of kindergarten were when he first invented the notion in 1837. When people think of kindergarten based on the school they may have attended as a child, they don't see the full scope of what Froebel had in mind. For Froebel, kindergarten was not just a first year of school with a special name that came before the child entered first grade; it was a learning experience that was to begin while the child was still in his or her mother's arms. He had witnessed young mothers at play with their children, listened to the songs they sang, and observed finger play, with which mothers stimulated their child's language skills and manual dexterity. He was among the first educational theorists to recognize the mother's role as the child's first teacher and the importance that she be trained to impart the best of learning to her children.

Women as Teachers

Froebel's observation of the special bond between mother and child led later to his most successful book on education, *Mother Play*, which consisted of songs and finger play (think of "The Itsy Bitsy Spider"—songs with accompanying finger motions) that mothers and children might do together and was intended to encourage young mothers to better grasp their important roles as their children's first real teachers, as well as engaging children in learning about their communities and themselves. In the development of kindergarten, Froebel placed tremendous emphasis on the role of women as teachers, particularly at the preschool and elementary school levels. Before

Froebel's Childhood

Froebel had come to his understanding of the mother's importance in the child's education through what was a rather hard path. His own mother had died when he was 9 months old. He was "shut up in a gloomy parsonage" and left in the care of a housemaid for much of the time. When young Froebel was 4, his father remarried. His new stepmother treated him with great love until her own child was born; at this point, he became an outcast, treated as a servant in his own home. The love between mother and child was a thing that he had received only for a very short time in his young life. Consequently, it would have been quite natural for Froebel to have had a curiosity about the relationship between mothers and their children.

Froebel's time, teaching was a nearly all-male profession, and anyone attempting to trace the history of women in education will discover Froebel and his kindergarten as revolutionary.

Figure C-1. A page from Froebel's book, *Mother Play*, shows the use of finger play and rhyming recitation put to music about fish swimming in the brook.

The Spread of Kindergarten

Froebel's invention of kindergarten has had a profound impact all around the world, despite the resistance that usually arises when new ideas and ideals disrupt the status quo. Even before Froebel's death in 1852, his methods were challenged by opponents and skeptics. In 1851, kindergartens were banned throughout Prussia until several years after Froebel's death. While the banning of kindergartens by the Kaiser was due largely to a misunderstanding in which Froebel's name was confused with that of his politically radical nephew, it was devastating for Froebel in his last years to have his invention outlawed by the state.

Following Froebel's death, the promotion of kindergarten was taken up in earnest by the Countess von Marenholtz-Bülow, who traveled, lectured, and wrote extensively and tirelessly to promote Froebel's ideas. Others took up the kindergarten cause, intrigued in part by the kindergarten gifts, but also by the joy that children seemed to

(continued on page 132)

Historically Speaking:

The Advancement of Kindergarten

"The Exposition kindergarten was conducted in an annex to the Woman's Pavilion, by Miss Ruth Burritt of Wisconsin, who had had several years of experience as a primary teacher before she became a kindergartner, and whose manner and insight were such as to gain adherents for the new cause. The enclosure for visitors was always crowded, many of the on-lookers being 'hewers of wood and drawers of water, who were attracted by the sweet singing and were spellbound by the lovely spectacle.' Thousands thronged to see the new educational departure, and many remained hours afterwards to ask questions.

The Exposition marked an epoch in the advancement of the kindergarten movement, as it marked an epoch in the history of elementary education. The ready acceptance of the kindergarten after the Philadelphia Exposition did not imply a recognition of its pedagogical value alone; in fact it is worthy of note that many of the kindergartens established at this period were philanthropic in their ultimate purpose. As the rapid growth of cities and the increasing immigration was fast developing the slum with its attendant evils, people were beginning to realize that some antidote must be found. The value of the kindergarten as a child-saving agency was at once recognized, and churches and philanthropic societies took up the movement.

The mere fact that the children of the slums were kept off the streets, and that they were made clean and happy by kind and motherly young women; that the child thus being cared for enabled the mother to go about her work in or outside the home — all this appealed to the heart of America, and America gave freely to make these kindergartens possible. Churches established kindergartens, individuals endowed kindergartens, and associations were organized for the spread and support of kindergartens in nearly every large city."

— Nina C. Vandewalker, 1908,
The Kindergarten in American Education

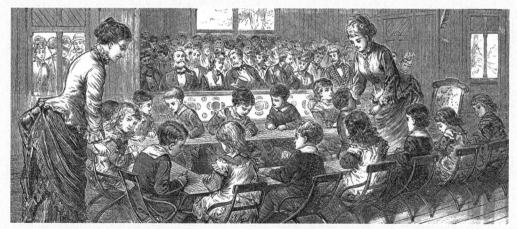

The kindergarten at the Philadelphia Centennial Exposition, 1876, from Frank Leslie's historical register of the United States Centennial by himself and Frank Norton.

find in the kindergarten style of learning. The first American kindergarten using Froebel's methods was started in Wisconsin in 1853. In Boston and other cities, philanthropists concerned with the huge influx of poor immigrants and the horrid conditions faced by the children of the poor started kindergartens as a way to help. The widespread introduction of kindergarten to the American public came through a model kindergarten in the Philadelphia Centennial Exposition in 1876.

The introduction of Froebel's kindergarten began gradually to have an effect on education at large. Even the great American educator John Dewey was deeply influenced by Froebel's kindergarten. In his laboratory school at the University of Chicago, Dewey said that "in a certain sense the school endeavors throughout its whole courses—now including children between four and thirteen—to carry into effect certain principles which Froebel was perhaps the first consciously to set forth."

Misapplication of Kindergarten

But as is the case with every new idea, some misunderstood kindergarten and rejected it, and others only partially understood kindergarten and misapplied its methods. When Froebel invented kindergarten, his schools were in small villages with very small class sizes, and with ample opportunity for walks in the woods, gardening, and nature studies. By the 1880s, Froebel's kindergartens in the U.S. numbered in the thousands, and the gifts of kindergarten were used in countries all around the world. But as kindergartens became institutionalized, most of the original ideas and ideals that came from Frobel were abandoned. The gifts and their wonders went the way of the dodo bird.

Historically Speaking:
The Appeal of Kindergarten

"The primary teacher who visited a kindergarten could not fail to be impressed by the kindergartner's attitude toward her children, by her cooperation with them in the spirit of comradeship and by her sympathetic insight into their interests and needs. She was impressed no less by the children's attitude toward their work, by the spontaneity of their interest, and by their delight in the use of the bright-colored material. The games were a revelation to her, since they showed that there could be freedom without disorder; the interest which the children took in the kindergarten songs made her own drill on scales and intervals seem little better than drudgery; and the attractiveness of the kindergarten room gave her helpful suggestions concerning the value of beauty as a factor in education. In short, recognizing that there was possible an order of things very different from that to which she was accustomed, she determined to profit by the lesson. If kindergarten procedure could be made so interesting, why not school procedure as well?"

—Nina C. Vandewalker, 1908, The
   Kindergarten in American Education

Historically Speaking:

Kindergarten as a Movement

"The kindergarten movement is one of the most significant movements in American education. In the fifty or more years that have passed since the first kindergarten was opened in the United States education has been transformed, and the kindergarten has been one of the agencies in the transformation. Although it came to this country when the educational ideal was still in the process of transformation, its aims and methods differed too radically from the prevailing ones to meet with immediate acceptance. The kindergarten is, however, the educational expression of the principles upon which American institutions are based, and as such it could not but live and grow upon American soil, if not in the school system, then out of it. Trusting to its inherent truth to win recognition and influence, it started on its educational mission as an independent institution, the embodiment of a new educational ideal. Its exponents proclaimed a new gospel—

that of man as a creative being, and education as a process of self-expression. They substituted activity for the prevailing repression, and insisted upon the child's right to himself and to happiness during the educational process. They emphasized the importance of early childhood, and made the ideal mother the standard for the teacher. They recognized the value of beauty as a factor in education, and by means of music, plants, and pictures in the kindergarten they revealed the barrenness of the old-time schoolroom. By their sympathetic interpretation of childhood, their exaltation of motherhood, their enthusiasm for humanity, and their intense moral earnestness they carried conviction to the educational world. The kindergarten so won its way to the hearts of the people that the school at last opened its doors and bade it welcome. It has become the symbol of the new education."

—Nina C. Vandewalker, 1908, The *Kindergarten in American Education*

Courtesy of Keene Public Library and the Historical Society of Cheshire, New Hampshire.

Photo C-1. While this photo shows lovely children sitting at their tables with their gift 3s, the instructor's table at the center and the expectation that all of the children would be doing what the instructor told them to do was not what Froebel had in mind for his gifts.

By the time that Maria Montessori developed her early childhood teaching techniques in Italy and launched an educational reform movement of her own, she was working in opposition to Italian kindergartens in which as many as 50 students were crowded into classrooms at one time. Here in the U.S., 30 students or more were gathered in kindergarten classes and expected to drill mindlessly through exercises with Froebel's gifts. **Photo C-1**, from Keen, Massachusetts, is particularly useful to understand the misapplication of Froebel's method at that time. Each child in the photo sits at the tables with their own set of blocks, gift 3, while at the center the teacher would demonstrate what the children were to do with their blocks. Waiting at the side might be two additional teaching assistants to help put the blocks away at the end of the lesson or to walk around and interfere with the children's exploration of Froebel's gifts. The gifts would have been more fruitfully explored in free play, one-on-one, or in much smaller groups between a parent or older sibling and child.

Froebel's Influence in the Scandinavian Countries

The influence of kindergarten was particularly strong in the Scandinavian countries, and while the gifts were available throughout the world at the time from educational supply manufacturers, most there were handcrafted within each small local community. For

instance, kindergarten gifts are still cherished in the Trøndelag Sverresborg Folk Museum in Trondheim, Norway (see **photos C-1** through **C-4**). Although kindergartens changed drastically in the U.S. and other countries, where such large numbers of children were managed in each class that Froebel would never have recognized them as kindergartens at all, Scandinavia, perhaps due to smaller populations of school children in small villages, seemed to have better kept Froebel's original gifts and ideas intact.

The Origins of Educational Sloyd

Perhaps equally important in Froebel's legacy was the manual arts training movement that grew from Scandinavia in the 1860s and 1870s. In 1860, the Russian Czar, who at that time was ruler of Finland, decided to reward the Finnish people for their good

(continued on page 136)

Photo C-2. Gifts 3, 4 and 6 in original handmade boxes in the Trøndelag Sverresborg Folk Museum.

Photo C-3. Gifts 3 and 4 used solo and in combination on display in the Trøndelag Sverresborg Folk Museum.

Historically Speaking:

The Original Kindergarten

A study of the original kindergartens under Froebel's own teaching or control seems to indicate that while he was in daily contact with the children, kindergarten procedure was much simpler and freer from technicalities than... later writings would lead us to believe. There were the gardens, excursions, walks, festivals, and the playing of games in the open air, which, all together, seem too loosely organized when compared with the average carefully systematized program of the present-day kindergartens in our large American cities. Definite changes in the program of the kindergarten seemed to follow when it was transplanted from the peasant localities and small villages with their yards, gardens, green fields and open meadows flooded with sunlight and affording ample room for healthful activity, into the crowded, modern city. Here the rooms used were originally intended for Sunday schools and churches, shops and stores, and school rooms only sufficiently large for the limited activities embodied in the narrow curriculum of that period. The rooms in which Froebel conducted his first schools and kindergartens were often poorly equipped, but the limited activities, light, and air were easily supplemented by the near-at-hand yards, gardens, village greens and meadows. The records of the activities of these early kindergartens when Froebel and the children were marching, singing and playing in the open air, as compared with conditions in many of our present-day kindergartens often remind one of the contrast between the strolling actors and singers of the Middle Ages, and the modern drama with its setting in artificial scenery and lights and the close, overheated atmosphere of the theatre.

—Pattie Smith Hill (1868–1946), *key founder of the National Association for Nursery Education*

Photo C-4. Paper weaving was nearly a universal expression of the kindergarten arts. These examples are from the Trøndelag Sverresborg Folk Museum.

Photo C-5. A historical photo displaying Froebel's construction gifts, including blocks of a much larger size. That all of the intricate constructions are in a relatively perfect form suggests that they were assembled by adults in staging this photo.

Historically Speaking:
Manual Training

Few among those currently associated with kindergarten or with career and technical education would remember that the training of the hand and eye through both kindergarten and the manual arts were once a common concern. In fact, when the manual training movement came to the United States in the late 1800s, it came in close collaboration with kindergarten. Both began to have a major impact on education through their introduction at the Philadelphia Centennial Exposition in 1876. There, acres of machine tools were set up, visitors attended a large display from Moscow that showed what would become known as the Russian system of manual arts training, and a model kindergarten was visited by an endless stream of visitors.

According to the editor's notes in the *Paradise of Childhood,* "The manual training exhibit sent from Russia to Philadelphia in 1876 began the evolution of a practical system of manual training in this country, and the corresponding exhibition of the kindergarten work and material, with the first practical kindergarten guide in the English language, was equally a forerunner of the kindergarten in America, which today stands well in advance of the work in all other parts of the world, while its possibilities can as yet be only imagined."

For many American educators and for educators worldwide, the movement to start kindergartens and the desire to begin manual training classes in schools were closely aligned. For many teachers, and particularly manual arts teachers, manual arts training was the best way to apply the kindergarten principles of self-activity to classes for children beyond the age for kindergarten. So it is natural for woodworkers to choose to make Froebel's gifts of childhood and to use what we do to advance the education of our kids.

behavior during the Crimean War (1853–1856) by building a national system of folk schools. A Lutheran priest, Uno Cygnaeus, was selected by the Czar's representatives to be in charge of building a school system where none had existed before. He first traveled all over Europe learning from the best schools and educators; he became convinced of the value of Froebel's kindergarten, but needed to build schools that went beyond kindergarten age. He determined to use craft education as the means to extend the kindergarten style of learning into the upper grades. To do so, he invented a system of manual arts training he called *sloyd*, which in Swedish meant "skilled or handy." Cygnaeus believed that handcrafts of various kinds would use Froebel's principle of self-activity to drive students, schools, and the national interest forward. Cygnaeus' invention of educational sloyd came during a time of rapid industrialization that brought cheap imported goods to the citizens of Scandinavia. Those same goods were undermining Scandinavian culture, which had been invested deeply in skilled home crafts, so Cygnaeus' invention quickly caught on. Educational sloyd programs

Historically Speaking:

Elementary Sloyd

The book *Elementary Sloyd and Whittling* by Gustaf Larsson, first published in 1906, is an excellent source for woodworking projects to use as occupations. For an introduction to the concept, here is an excerpt from Jean Lee Hunt's 1918 *Catalog of Play Equipment.*

THE CARPENTER BENCH

The carpenter equipment must be a "sure-enough business affair," and the tools real tools—not toys.

The Sheldon bench shown here is a real bench in every particular except size. The tool list is as follows:

- Manual training hammer.
- 18 point cross-cut saw.
- 9 point rip saw.
- Large screw driver, wooden handle.
- Small screw driver.
- Nail puller.
- Stanley smooth-plane, No. 3.
- Bench hook.
- Brace and set of twist bits.
- Manual training rule.
- Steel rule.
- Tri square.
- Utility box—with assorted nails, screws, etc.
- Combination India oil stone.
- Oil can.
- Small hatchet.

Choice of lumber must be determined partly by the viewpoint of the adult concerned, largely by the laboratory budget, and finally by the supply locally available. Excellent results have sometimes been achieved where only boxes from the grocery and left-over pieces from the carpenter shop have been provided. Such rough lumber affords good experience in manipulation, and its use may help to establish habits of adapting materials as we find them to the purposes we have in hand. This is the natural attack of childhood, and it should be fostered, for children can lose it and come to feel that specially prepared materials are essential, and a consequent limitation to ingenuity and initiative can thus be established.

On the other hand, some projects and certain stages of experience are best served by a supply of good regulation stock. Boards of soft pine, white wood, bass wood, or cypress in thicknesses of ¼", ⅜", ½" and ⅞" are especially well adapted for children's work, and "stock strips" ¼" and ½" thick and 2" and 3" wide lend themselves to many purposes.

Girl at a carpenter bench.

were launched throughout the Baltic/ Scandinavian region, putting handcrafts at the center of children's education.

The Similarity of Educational Sloyd to Froebel's Occupations

What had been invented in Finland by Uno Cygnaeus was taken up and promoted throughout the world (including the U.S.) by Otto Salomon in Sweden, and the system of manual arts education based on the teaching methods of Friedrich Froebel became known as *Swedish sloyd*. This was a natural extension of Froebel's idea of occupations. And like Froebel's occupations, sloyd was not intended to make tradesmen of the students or to fit and prepare them for specific jobs within their communities, but worked from the realization of the important relationship between the use of the hands and the development of intelligence. What one might learn in the occupation of wood shop would be useful in fields far beyond the craft of woodworking. Swedish sloyd was a natural extension of self-activity; students older than those in kindergarten were given real tools and real materials, along with the opportunity to make useful beauty from wood. A special emphasis was placed on making well-crafted objects that would serve to strengthen the bonds between home and school, and to help the child to understand his or her important role in the sustenance of human culture and community life.

The Present

Though sloyd was successfully integrated into American public schools for many years, in the 1980s educational policy makers began eliminating woodworking education and the number of wood shops began to decline. Kindergartens continued to occupy a place in American schools as the year before first grade began, but with much of what Froebel intended stripped from it.

Perhaps Froebel's greatest gift to parents, educators, and children was his recognition of the value of play. When my mother was a kindergarten teacher in Omaha, Nebraska's public schools, she would tell the parents of her kids, "When you ask your child, 'What did you did in school today?' and what your child says is 'Play,' please know that play is much more than play. It's how a child learns." In the drive to standardize education and pressure our children toward some form of "success," we have forgotten the value of self-activity, and that play is essential to learning. It is my hope that by remembering Friedrich Froebel, and by engaging in the making of his gifts, we can restore greater meaning, greater skill, greater creativity, and more effective learning to the lives of our children.

Resources

An incredible set of resources is available free online and can be downloaded. A more recent and inspirational text is *Inventing Kindergarten* by Norm Brosterman. Another important resource is Froebelweb.org. Ready-made kindergarten gifts can be purchased from redhentoys.com. The following books and resources are recommended for those readers seeking more information on Froebel's methods and history, as well as childhood development.

Froebel and Education Through Self-Activity by H. Courthope Bowen

Froebel as a Pioneer in Modern Psychology by Elsie Riach Murray

Hand Work and Head Work by Bertha von Marenholtz-Bülow

Inventing Kindergarten by Norm Brosterman

Papers on Froebel, with Suggestions on Principles and Methods of Child Culture in Different Countries by Henry Barnard

Songs and Music of Froebel's Mother Play prepared and arranged by Susan Blow

Symbolic Education by Susan Blow

The Kindergarten Building Gifts by Elizabeth Harrison

The Kindergarten Guide by Lois Bates

The Kindergarten in American Education by Nina C. Vandewalker

The Kindergarten Movement in Wisconsin by Nina C. Vandewalker

The New Education by Work, According to Froebel's Method by Bertha von Marenholtz-Bülow

The Paradise of Childhood by Edward Weibé

United Kindergarten and First-Grade Teaching by Samuel Chester Parker and Alice Temple

About the Author

Photo by Rod Slane

Doug Stowe began his woodworking career in 1976, and founded the Eureka Springs Guild of Artists and Craftspeople in 1977.

In 1995, he started writing books and articles about woodworking. In 1998, he was one of three founders of the Eureka Springs School of the Arts.

In 2001, he started the *Wisdom of the Hands* Program at the Clear Spring School, a small independent school in Eureka Springs, Arkansas, to prove the value of wood shop and hands-on learning. Continuing that effort, in 2006 he began his blog, Wisdom of the Hands. His work with wood and in education led the Arkansas Arts Council to name Doug an Arkansas Living Treasure in 2009.

He has published more than 70 articles in various woodworking magazines and educational journals and has written 10 books on woodworking techniques.

Doug continues to teach woodworking for grades 1–12 at the Clear Spring School, to work daily in his own shop, and to travel around the country teaching adult woodworking classes for schools and clubs.

He lives in a hardwood forest at the edge of Eureka Springs, Arkansas, with his wife, Jean.

"Making beautiful and useful things from wood and sharing the experience with others makes for a meaningful life."
–Doug Stowe

Acknowledgements

My sincere thanks and appreciation are offered to the folks at Spring House Press who took my step-by-step photos, text, and reflections and wove them together into coherent form. You will find their names listed in the credits at the beginning of this book.

I have been nudged along the way in the writing of this book by readers of my blog, Wisdom of the Hands, and by a mother who was a kindergarten teacher in the good old days when the child's primary responsibilities were to play and learn to get along with each other.

To all those who've helped me on this journey, I offer thanks.

Index

CPSIA information can be obtained
at www.ICGtesting.com
Printed in the USA
JSHW041950160623
43358JS00008B/20